Ga... ...l

SUP...

Ful... ...ed

3 in 1

Up

JIM DAVIS

RAVETTE BOOKS

First published by
Ravette Books Limited 1994

Printed and bound in Great Britain
for Ravette Books Limited,
P.O. Box 296
Horsham, West Sussex RH13 8FH
An Egmont Company
by Cox & Wyman Ltd, Reading

ISBN: 1 85304 818 6

Garfield
In The Pink

JIM DAVIS

I THINK I'LL WRITE A BOOK THIS WEEK. THEY SAY EVERYONE HAS A GOOD BOOK IN THEM
JIM DAVIS
3-10
© 1986 United Feature Syndicate, Inc.
I MAY HAVE AN ENTIRE LIBRARY

IN ORDER TO WRITE A BOOK I MUST GO OUT AND LIVE LIFE
JIM DAVIS
3-11
I THINK I'LL RUN WITH THE BULLS IN PAMPLONA!
THEN I'LL WRITE A BOOK ENTITLED "THE STUPIDEST THING I'VE EVER DONE"
© 1986 United Feature Syndicate, Inc.

WE WRITERS HAVE AN UNCANNY ABILITY TO OBSERVE OURSELVES FROM AN OMNISCIENT POINT OF VIEW
JIM DAVIS
3-12
"AS THE HANDSOME CAT GAZED UPON THE FOLLY OF LIFE ABOUT HIM HE TOSSED HIS HEAD BACK IN LAUGHTER... HA! HA! HA!"
AND THEN HE FELL RIGHT OFF HIS CHAIR
© 1986 United Feature Syndicate, Inc.

SOME PEOPLE ONLY TALK ABOUT WRITING BOOKS
JIM DAVIS
3-13
AND SOME PEOPLE DO SOMETHING ABOUT IT
YES...YES, THIS IS HOW I WANT TO BE PHOTOGRAPHED FOR THE BOOK JACKET
© 1986 United Feature Syndicate, Inc.

GO AHEAD AND EAT, JON. I'M A WRITER. I'LL SIT HERE AND OBSERVE YOU
© 1986 United Feature Syndicate,Inc.
I THINK I'LL WRITE AN AUTOBIOGRAPHY!
JIM DAVIS 3-14

I MUST SUFFER IN ORDER TO WRITE A GREAT NOVEL
WHANG!
© 1986 United Feature Syndicate, Inc.
THANK YOU, JON. I'LL REMEMBER YOU IN MY ACCEPTANCE SPEECH FOR THE NOBEL PRIZE FOR LITERATURE
JIM DAVIS 3-15

ISN'T RAIN WONDERFUL, GARFIELD?
WHEN IT STOPS, THE EARTH IS CLEANSED AND THE PLANTS ARE REFRESHED
AND I GET TO GO OUT ON THE DRIVEWAY AND STOMP ON EARTHWORMS
JIM DAVIS 2·26
© 1988 United Feature Syndicate, Inc.

UH-OH!
JIM DAVIS
2-27
JON SHOULD NEVER LEAVE HIS BUNNY SLIPPERS UNDER THE BED ALONE
© 1986 United Feature Syndicate, Inc.

ODIE, YOU WERE A BAD BOY FOR CHEWING ON THE SOFA
JIM DAVIS
2-28

TAP
TAP
TAP

IS THIS A PRIVATE PARTY, OR CAN ANYONE PLAY?

WHAM!
WHAM!
WHAM!
WHAM!
WHAM!
GARFIELD
JIM DAVIS 3-1

GLOP!

THE SERVICE HERE IS SLOW, BUT AT LEAST THE WAITER IS RUDE
GARFIELD

SIGH
JIM DAVIS
1-27

GRAVITY

WHY FIGHT IT?
© 1986 United Feature Syndicate, Inc.

IT'S FUN TO LIE HERE AND MUSE ON THE MEANING OF LIFE,
JIM DAVIS
1-28
AND MUSE ON THE MYRIAD OF SOLUTIONS TO THE WORLD'S WOES,
AND TO COUNT THE CRACKS IN THE CEILING
© 1986 United Feature Syndicate, Inc.

PEOPLE SEEM TO BE LEADING MORE ACTIVE LIFESTYLES THESE DAYS
JIM DAVIS
1-29

I WONDER WHAT THAT WOULD BE LIKE?

THE ONLY THING ACTIVE ABOUT ME IS MY IMAGINATION
© 1986 United Feature Syndicate,Inc.

HEY, GARFIELD, GUESS WHAT? WE ARE GOING TO VISIT DAD AND MOM ON THE FARM AGAIN!
4-14
JIM DAVIS
JON, YOU MUST BE PSYCHIC
I WAS JUST LYING HERE THINKING IT WAS TIME TO RESTOCK THE BURRS IN MY FUR

HEY, MOM, PASS THE POTATOES, PLEASE
SCALLOPED, WHIPPED, FRIED, BAKED OR BOILED?
MOM, YOU ALWAYS FIX TOO MUCH FOOD
I KNOW, HONEY, I KNOW. NOW, WHAT WOULD YOU LIKE?
I CAN'T DECIDE. JUST GIVE ME A PIECE OF PIE
APPLE, PEACH, PUMPKIN, BLUEBERRY, CHERRY, OR BANANA CREAM?
4-13
JIM DAVIS

FARM LIFE'S GREAT, ISN'T IT, GARFIELD?
4-16
HOWEVER, I WILL ADMIT IT'S A LITTLE SLOW
NOTHING MUCH TO DO BUT COUNT THE BRICKS IN THE OLD SILO
14,238
JIM DAVIS

LOOK, GARFIELD! A MOO COW!
4-17
JIM DAVIS
AND A BOW-WOW!
AND A PIGGY-WIGGY!
© 1986 United Feature Syndicate, Inc.
HA-HA, YOU GUYS!
THIS MUST BE THE FAMOUS FARM HUMOR I'VE HEARD ABOUT

IT'S CLOUDIN' UP
YUP
JIM DAVIS
LOOKS LIKE RAIN
YUP
THESE ARE MEN OF FEW WORDS
© 1986 United Feature Syndicate, Inc.
4-19
IT'S RAININ'
YUP
AND FEW BRAINS

JIM DAVIS
KIND OF MUDDY TODAY, ISN'T IT, GARFIELD?
IT IS
4-18
IT'S TOO DEEP FOR A LITTLE FELLER LIKE YOU
I KNOW
© 1986 United Feature Syndicate, Inc.
YOU OUGHTA GET UP ON JON'S SHOULDERS
I AM

THE NEWSPAPER SHOULD BE HERE ABOUT NOW
4-21
JIM DAVIS
BONK!
© 1986 United Feature Syndicate, Inc.
SOMETIMES YOU GET THE PAPER, SOMETIMES THE PAPER GETS YOU

MY LIFE IS BORING
JIM DAVIS
4-22
HAVE YOU HEARD THE OLD SAYING, "ALL DRESSED UP AND NO PLACE TO GO"?
I'M NAKED AND NO PLACE TO GO

I GOTTA DO SOMETHING TO SPICE UP MY LIFE
JIM DAVIS
I KNOW! I'LL TAKE MY AFTERNOON NAP IN THE MORNING AND MY MORNING NAP IN THE AFTERNOON
© 1986 United Feature Syndicate, Inc.
GARFIELD, YOU MAD, IMPETUOUS BOY, YOU
4-23

LIFE IS LIKE A FERRARI. IT GOES TOO FAST
BUT THAT'S OKAY
© 1986 United Feature Syndicate, Inc.
BECAUSE YOU CAN'T AFFORD IT ANYWAY
JIM DAVIS
4-24

I SHALL NOW MEDITATE IN ORDER TO ENRICH MY LIFE
4-25
JIM DAVIS
THERE IS NOTHING LIKE MEDITATION TO GET IN TOUCH WITH ONE'S SELF
© 1986 United Feature Syndicate, Inc.
SELF... IF YOU DON'T GET OUT OF THIS STUPID POSITION IN ABOUT THREE SECONDS, YOUR KNEECAPS ARE GOING TO FALL OFF!

LIFE IS LIKE A BIRDBATH. IT'S MADE OF CONCRETE, FILLED WITH WATER, AND UH... BIRDS LIKE TO SPLASH IN IT
BOY, THAT WAS DUMB. LIFE ISN'T ANYTHING LIKE A BIRDBATH
TAP TAP
© 1986 United Feature Syndicate, Inc.
LIFE... IS LIKE A SOCK MONKEY...
JIM DAVIS 4-26

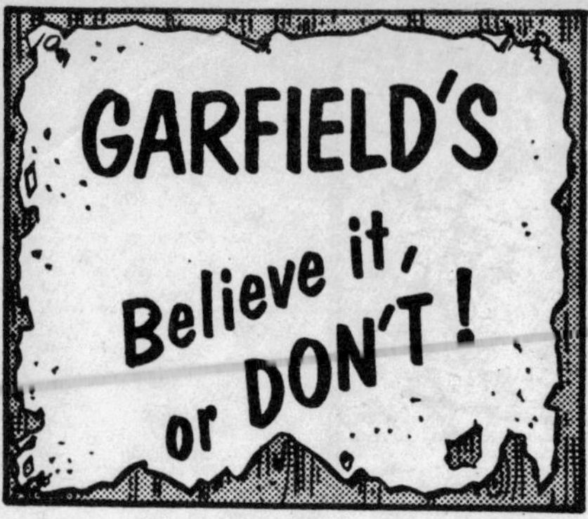
GARFIELD'S
Believe it, or DON'T!

A JON ARBUCKLE CLAIMS TO OWN A CAT WHO CAN EAT 10 TIMES ITS BODY WEIGHT. TO VERIFY HIS CLAIM WE OFFERED THE CAT 270 POUNDS OF LASAGNA
© 1986 United Feature Syndicate, Inc.

THE CAT ATE ONLY 219 POUNDS OF LASAGNA
THINGS WENT SO WELL IN REHEARSAL
Believe it, or DON'T!
JIM DAVIS
1-21

LET'S SEE HOW MUCH YOU KNOW ABOUT CATS
JIM DAVIS
HERE ARE TWO PEOPLE WHO, FOR ALL PRACTICAL PURPOSES, APPEAR TO BE IDENTICAL
© 1985 United Feature Syndicate, Inc.
1-9-86
GUESS WHICH ONE IS ALLERGIC TO CATS

I WONDER IF THAT FLOOR IS COLD
1-10-86
JIM DAVIS
© 1985 United Feature Syndicate, Inc.
YUP... IT'S COLD ALL RIGHT

I LOVE HANGING ON THE SCREEN DOOR. I CAN BE A FLY OR A MOUNTAIN CLIMBER...
♪
ACME
WHAM! WHAM! WHAM!
© 1985 United Feature Syndicate, Inc.
1-11-86
OR A DOOR KNOCKER
♪
JIM DAVIS

I HATE PARTLY CLOUDY DAYS
JIM DAVIS 4-7
WHEN IT'S SUNNY, I'M HAPPY. WHEN IT'S CLOUDY, I'M SAD
© 1986 United Feature Syndicate, Inc.
ON A PARTLY CLOUDY DAY I CAN USE UP A WEEK'S WORTH OF MOODS

MY, MY. YOU'RE UP EARLY THIS MORNING
I DIDN'T GET UP EARLY
MY LEG CRAMP DID!
JIM DAVIS 4-8
© 1986 United Feature Syndicate, Inc.

I HATE IT WHEN I CAN'T GET MILK CARTONS OPEN
LET ME GIVE YOU A HAND
MILK
JIM DAVIS
4-9
HIYAH!
THOCK!
MILK
© 1986 United Feature Syndicate, Inc.
AMAZING THINGS: CLAWS
MILK

GARFIELD, YOU PROWL ALL NIGHT AND YOU SLEEP ALL DAY. YOU ALSO EAT TOO MUCH
JIM DAVIS

WHAT DO YOU HAVE TO SAY FOR YOURSELF?

YOU ONLY GO AROUND NINE TIMES IN LIFE, SO GRAB FOR ALL THE GUSTO YOU CAN GET
3-17

GARFIELD, IT'S TIME TO PUT YOU ON ANOTHER DIET
ARRRGH!
JIM DAVIS

DO YOU KNOW WHAT A DIET COULD DO TO ME?

I COULD WASTE AWAY TO NORMAL!
3-18

JIM DAVIS
THE T V ADVERTISERS DIDN'T WASTE ANY TIME
© United Feature Syndicate, Inc.
I'VE BEEN ON A DIET ONE DAY AND THEY'RE ALREADY RUNNING MORE FOOD COMMERCIALS
3-19

WHY IS IT I ALWAYS HAVE TO GO ON DIETS?
3-24
JIM DAVIS
OH, SURE, I'VE PUT ON A POUND OR TWO...
OR THREE OR FOUR OR FIVE
© 1986 United Feature Syndicate, Inc.

HERE'S YOUR DIET SALAD, GARFIELD
3-25

WOULD YOU LIKE ANYTHING ON IT?
IF YOU DON'T MIND

PERHAPS YOU COULD GARNISH IT WITH A CHOCOLATE CAKE
JIM DAVIS

3-26
JIM DAVIS

I THINK I KNOW HOW ODIE STAYS SO SLIM

IT MUST TAKE A LOT OF ENERGY TO BE THAT STUPID
RRRRRR
© 1986 United Feature Syndicate, Inc.

YOU HAVE LOST THREE POUNDS
3-27
CONGRATULATIONS, GARFIELD!
THANK, YOU
© 1986 United Feature Syndicate, Inc.
PSSST, WHEN DO I GET MY FRESH BATTERIES?
LATER
JIM DAVIS

GARFIELD, IN ORDER TO SUCCESSFULLY DIET, YOU MUST CHANGE YOUR EATING HABITS
GARFIELD
3-28
JIM DAVIS
© 1986 United Feature Syndicate, Inc.
ARFIELD
SPLUT!
ARFIELD

ON WHICH DAY ARE MOST DIETS BEGUN?
3-29
WRONG. MONDAY IS THE SECOND MOST POPULAR DAY
© 1986 United Feature Syndicate, Inc.
JIM DAVIS
MOST DIETS ARE BEGUN "TOMORROW"

YOU SHOULDN'T WATCH SAD MOVIES WHEN YOU'RE ON A DIET, GARFIELD. YOU KNOW HOW EMOTIONAL YOU GET
JIM DAVIS
THIS ISN'T A SAD MOVIE
© 1986 United Feature Syndicate, Inc.
IT'S A FOOD COMMERCIAL
3-22

I'D LIKE TO BE ABLE TO STOP EACH OF THOSE CARS AND ASK THE PEOPLE WHERE THEY'RE GOING. IF THEY DIDN'T HAVE A GOOD EXCUSE I'D SEND THEM HOME
JIM DAVIS
5-28
OF COURSE, SOME OF THEM MAY NOT HAVE A HOME... HOW SAD
"CAR PEOPLE"

THE BIRDS SEEM TO BE SINGING MORE THIS TIME OF YEAR
CHIRP CHIRP
TWEET
JIM DAVIS
THEY MAY BE HERALDING A CHANGE IN SEASONS
TWEET
© 1988 United Feature Syndicate, Inc.
5-29
THEN AGAIN, IT COULD BE THE SHOWER JON INSTALLED IN THE BIRDBATH
TWEET

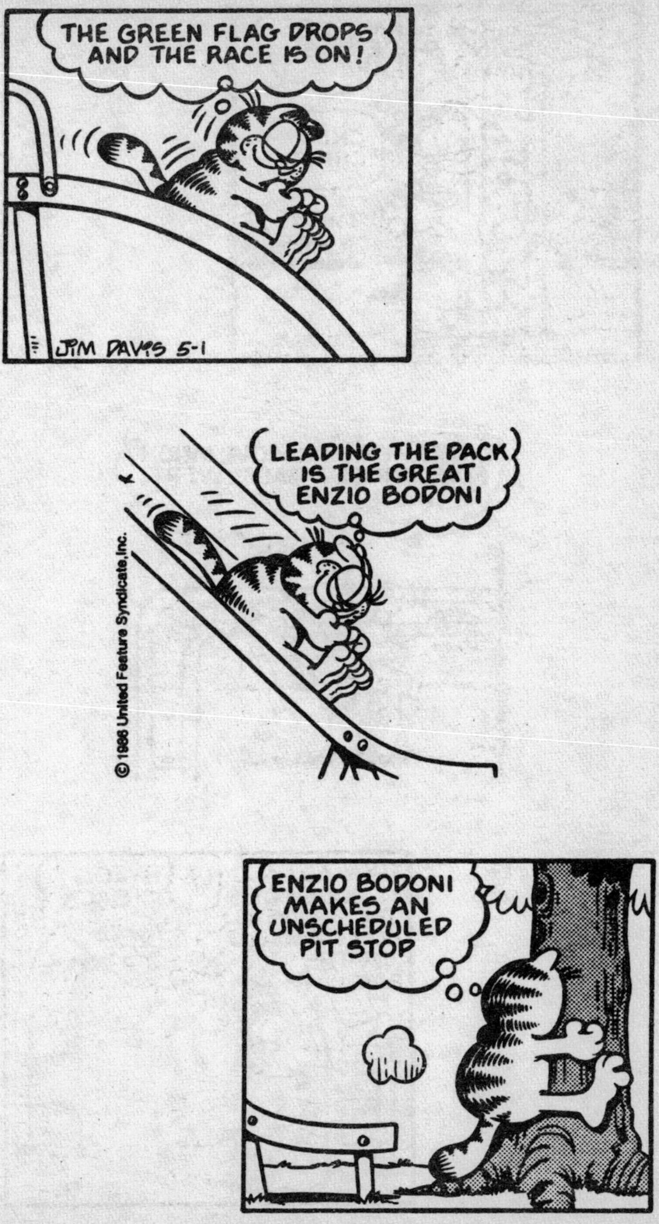
THE GREEN FLAG DROPS AND THE RACE IS ON!
JIM DAVIS 5-1
LEADING THE PACK IS THE GREAT ENZIO BODONI
ENZIO BODONI MAKES AN UNSCHEDULED PIT STOP

GEE, I LOVE PLAYGROUNDS
5-2
I REMEMBER HOW MUCH FUN MONKEY BARS WERE WHEN I WAS A KID
© 1988 United Feature Syndicate, Inc.
I GUESS YOU CAN'T GO BACK
JIM DAVIS

ODIE, I NEED YOUR HELP
JPM DAVIS
LET'S PLAY ON THE TEETER-TOTTER
I COULD JUST CRY
5-3

6-2

LITTER BOX PACKED UP?
I HATE MONDAYS
JIM DAVIS

YIP! YIP! YIP!
LET ME HELP YOU, ODIE
6-3
PLOOP!
I DON'T KNOW HOW YOU DOGS SURVIVE
UH... JON?
COOKIES
JIM DAVIS

ARE YOU GOING TO EAT THAT HAMBURGER, POOKY?
6-4
I LOVE EATING WITH TEDDY BEARS
© 1988 United Feature Syndicate, Inc.
THEY'RE ALWAYS STUFFED
JIM DAVIS

6-5
JIM DAVIS
GARFIELD
GARFIELD! DIN...
GULP!
ZIP!
GARFIELD
© 1986 United Feature Syndicate, Inc.
URP...WHAT'S ON TV?
COME BACK HERE AND LINGER!
GARFIELD

TAPPITY
TAPPITY
TAPPITY

I KNEW A DOG WHO
WAS SO STUPID, HE CHASED
BONES AND BURIED CARS!
JIM DAVIS
6-6
© 1986 United Feature Syndicate, Inc.

CLONK!
BONK!
BOP!
BAP!

I KNEW A DOG WHO WAS SO RICH, HE HIRED SOMEONE TO DROOL FOR HIM!
6-7
HA! HA! HA! HA!
I HATE TO LAUGH AT MY OWN JOKES
JIM DAVIS

HOW'S YOUR COFFEE THIS MORNING, GARFIELD?
A LITTLE WEAK
THUD!
© 1986 United Feature Syndicate, Inc.
SEE? IT DIDN'T EVEN CRACK THE PLATE
JIM DAVIS
7-28

GOBBLE MUNCH SMACK SLURP
© 1986 United Feature Syndicate, Inc.
BURP
JIM DAVIS 7-29

YAWN
7-21
JIM DAVIS

© 1986 United Feature Syndicate, Inc.

MONDAYS ARE LOSING THEIR SUBTLETY

MONDAY
21
JIM DAVIS
7-22
RIP
MONDAY
22
OH, NO! IT'S THE MONDAY THAT WOULDN'T DIE!
MONDAY
22

YOU'RE RIGHT, GARFIELD. EVERY DAY THIS WEEK IS MONDAY
MONDAY 23
MONDAY 21
I'M SURE IT'S JUST A MISPRINT. IT DOESN'T MEAN ANYTHING
MONDAY 23
MONDAY 21
© 1988 United Feature Syndicate, Inc.
THEN AGAIN
GONK!
MONDAY

GARFIELD'S
Believe it, or DON'T!
A CAT IN LUBBOCK, TEXAS GAVE BIRTH TO 57 KITTENS
© 1986 United Feature Syndicate, Inc.
WHEN ASKED HOW SHE FELT AFTER GIVING BIRTH TO QUINSEPTUPLETS, SHE SAID:
I'LL FEEL BETTER WHEN THEY START SLEEPING THROUGH THE NIGHT
JPM DAVPS 1·25
Believe it, or DON'T!

THIS IS FOR YOU
MAIL?! FOR ME?! WOW! I'M IMPORTANT! I'M SOMEBODY
JIM DAVIS 1-4-86
HEY, WAIT A MINUTE! THIS IS ADDRESSED TO "OCCUPANT"!
ARE YOU READY FOR LUNCH, "OCCUPANT"?
THAT'S **MISTER** OCCUPANT TO YOU

IT'S JUST ABOUT TIME...
JIM DAVIS
12-30
SPLUT!
YUP, THERE'S THE 8:25 PIE RIGHT ON SCHEDULE
© 1985 United Feature Syndicate, Inc.

SPLUT
ODI
WHAP! WHAP! WHAP! WHAP!
WHAT WAS THAT ALL ABOUT?
I'M TRAINING YOU GUYS TO HATE MONDAYS TOO
JIM DAVIS
8-11

MAYBE I SHOULD CUT DOWN ON COFFEE
IT'S STARTING TO KEEP ME AWAKE
© 1986 United Feature Syndicate, Inc.
I MUST HAVE TOSSED AND TURNED FOR THREE MINUTES LAST NIGHT
8-12
JIM DAVIS

SLUCK
JIM DAVIS
DONK!
8-13
© 1986 United Feature Syndicate, Inc.
NOTHING SPOILS LUNCH ANY QUICKER THAN A ROGUE MEATBALL RAMPAGING THROUGH YOUR SPAGHETTI

HEY, GARFIELD. COME HERE
JIM DAVIS 8-14
I'M SLEEPING WITH MY SOCKS ON TONIGHT
© 1986 United Feature Syndicate, Inc.
HEE HEE
HAR! HAR! LIFE IS A GAS WHEN YOU LIVE WITH A CRAZY MAN LIKE JON!

PANT
PANT
PANT
8-15
© 1986 United Feature Syndicate, Inc.
SCRIT
JIM DAVIS

HMMM
GARFIELD
CAT FOOD
Ingredients: You're better off not knowing.
CAT FOOD
GARFIE
JIM DAVIS
8-16
© 1986 United Feature Syndicate, Inc.
WHAT YOU DON'T KNOW CAN'T HURT YOU, RIGHT?
GARFIEL
CAT FOOD

WHEW! BOY IS MY BREATH BAD THIS MORNING
JIM DAVIS
IT MUST HAVE BEEN THAT SANDWICH I ATE BEFORE BED LAST NIGHT
OR POSSIBLY THAT BLOCK OF GOAT CHEESE
9-29

I GOTTA FIND SOMETHING FOR THIS BAD BREATH
AHA!
© 1986 United Feature Syndicate,Inc.
YOUR BREATH SMELLS FUNNY
YOURS WOULD TOO IF YOU GARGLED WITH AFTER-SHAVE
JIM DAVIS
9-30

THERE'S ALL KINDS OF NEAT STUFF IN HERE
DEODORANT. I KNOW WHAT THIS IS FOR
10-1
United Feature Syndicate, Inc.
SSSSSSS
GARFIELD
JIM DAVIS

BZZZZ
JIM DAVIS
10-2
CLICK
© 1988 United Feature Syndicate, Inc.
PLAYING WITH MY ELECTRIC RAZOR, GARFIELD?
NEVER MIND

GARFIELD!
JIM DAVIS
10-3
YOU'RE USING MY TOOTHBRUSH!
STICK AROUND. YOU CAN WATCH ME FLOSS
© 1986 United Feature Syndicate, Inc.
IS NOTHING SACRED?!
WHERE'S THAT MOUTHWASH?

RATS, WHAT HAPPENED TO THE MAPLE SYRUP?

NOW I REMEMBER... THE SYRUP BOTTLE SPRANG A LEAK
SYRU
10-4

SO I POURED IT IN JON'S HAIR TONIC BOTTLE
SYRU
JIM DAVIS

Z
CRASH!
DONK!
WHAP!
© 1986 United Feature Syndicate, Inc.
THE MONDAY PAPER
JIM DAVIS 10-13

JIM DAVIS 10-14
WHY, HELLO, GARFIELD. WHERE HAVE YOU BEEN ALL DAY?
PURRR
© 1988 United Feature Syndicate, Inc.
UNDER YOUR CAR

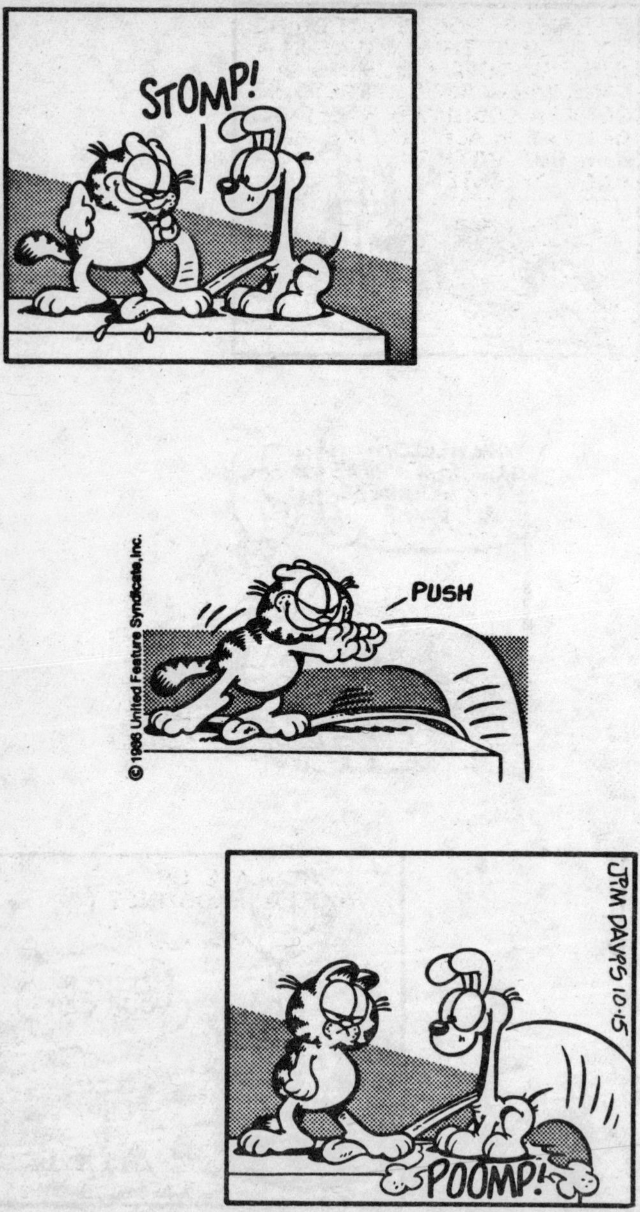
STOMP!
© 1986 United Feature Syndicate, Inc.
PUSH
JIM DAVIS 10-15
POOMP!

GARFIELD! YOU'RE NOT GOING TO BELIEVE THIS! I WAS IN A BAKERY TODAY BUYING A CAKE WHEN THREE MIDGETS IN GORILLA COSTUMES RACED IN, SET THE PLACE ON FIRE AND RAN OUT WITH THE CASH REGISTER!
WOW!
COME ON, JON. DON'T SPARE THE DETAILS!
© 1988 United Feature Syndicate, Inc.
CHOCOLATE OR VANILLA FROSTING?
JIM DAVIS 10-16

TODAY I WILL DEMONSTRATE "DEEP-KNEE-KRICKS"
JIM DAVIS 10-17
THIS IS ONE I'M SURE JUST ABOUT ALL OF YOU CAN DO
© 1986 United Feature Syndicate, Inc.
KRICK
KRICK

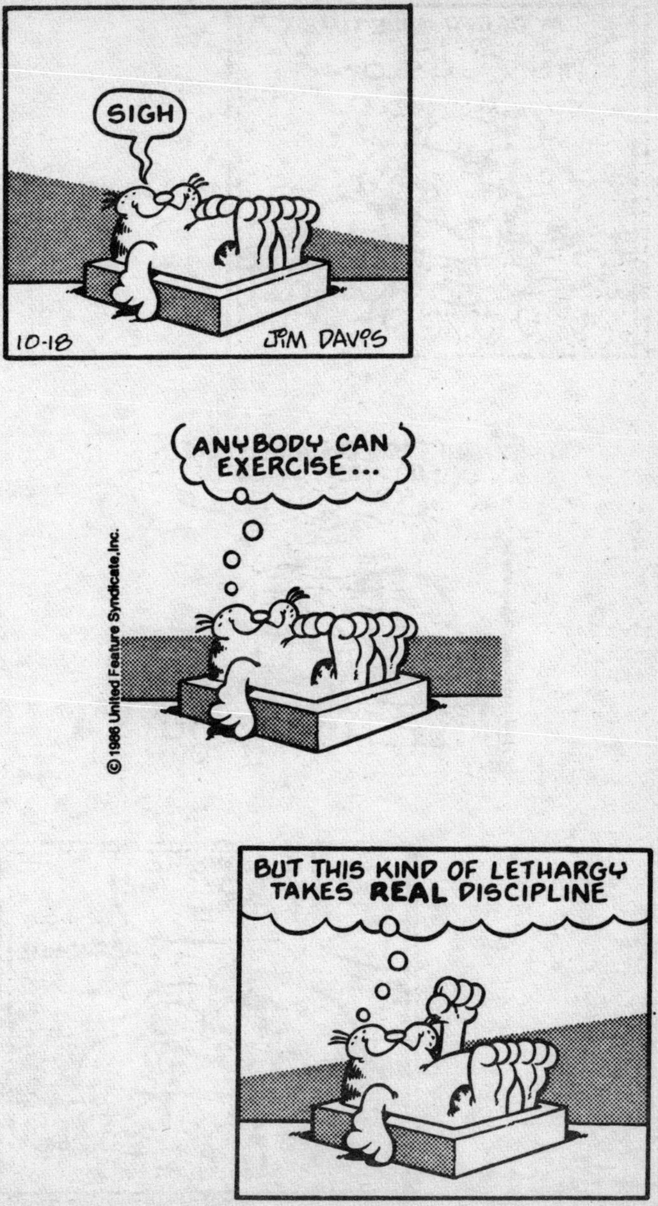
SIGH
10-18
JIM DAVIS
ANYBODY CAN EXERCISE...
BUT THIS KIND OF LETHARGY TAKES REAL DISCIPLINE

I'M READY THIS TIME
JIM DAVIS 10-20

COME ON, MONDAY. DO YOUR WORST

GARFIELD, WE'RE GOING TO SEE THE VET TODAY
ARRRGHH!

TELL ME SOMETHING, DOC
WHY IS IT EVERY TIME I BRING A HOUSEPLANT HOME, GARFIELD EATS IT?
GIVEN THE SHAPE HE'S IN, IT'S ONE OF THE FEW THINGS IN HIS DIET THAT CAN'T OUTRUN HIM
SHE'S A FUNNY LADY
JIM DAVIS 10-21

GIVE ME ONE GOOD REASON WHY YOU WON'T GO OUT WITH ME, DOC
YOU'RE OBNOXIOUS, PUSHY, WISHY-WASHY, SLOW-WITTED AND BORING
OH YEAH? WELL GIVE ME A SECOND REASON
JIM DAVIS 10-22

HOW OLD IS YOUR CAT, MR. ARBUCKLE?
HE'S EIGHT
REALLY? HE DOESN'T LOOK THAT OLD
© 1986 United Feature Syndicate, Inc.
HE SHOULDN'T. HE'S ONLY BEEN AWAKE FOR ABOUT TWO OF THOSE YEARS
IS IT ANY WONDER I HATE HIM?
JIM DAVIS 10-25

JUST WHAT WOULD I HAVE TO DO TO GET YOU TO GO OUT WITH ME, DOC?
STAND ON YOUR HEAD AND SCREAM LIKE A CHICKEN, FOR STARTERS
BUCK-BUCK-BUC-KAW!
DIGNITY IS NOT IN THIS MAN'S VOCABULARY
JIM DAVIS 10-25
© 1986 United Feature Syndicate, Inc.

LOOK, JON. MY BOYFRIEND WOULDN'T LIKE IT IF HE KNEW YOU WERE TRYING TO ASK ME OUT
OH, YEAH? WHAT'S HIS NAME
NICK "THE MANGLER" SCARLOTTI
OOOO! I'M IMPRESSED!
© 1986 United Feature Syndicate, Inc.
JIM DAVIS 10-24
I AM IMPRESSED

GO! GO! GO!
GARFIELD, THAT MONSTER SHARK JUST ATE TOKYO. WHY ARE YOU CHEERING FOR IT?
© 1986 United Feature Syndicate, Inc
ANYTHING THAT EATS EVERYTHING CAN'T BE ALL BAD
JIM DAVIS
11-3

JIM DAVIS 11-4

AND WHAT ARE YOU SUPPOSED TO BE?

ANOTHER HAPLESS BATHER FALLS PREY TO THE TIGER SHARK

THE CUNNING TIGER SHARK, THE WORLD'S MOST EFFICIENT EATING MACHINE WITH THE WORLD'S MOST VORACIOUS APPETITE, SPIES A HELPLESS FEAST!
JIM DAVIS 11-5
FEEDING FRENZY!
YUCK! ANCHOVIES!
PTOO!

I SUPPOSE YOU THINK YOU LOOK LIKE A SHARK
YOU GOT IT, BUSTER
JIM DAVIS 11-6
WELL YOU DON'T LOOK ANYTHING LIKE A SHARK!
OH, YEAH?
WELL JUST WAIT UNTIL MY FIN COMES BACK FROM THE CLEANERS!

MUNCH
CHOMP
GULP
© 1986 United Feature Syndicate,Inc.
JUST WHEN YOU THOUGHT IT WAS SAFE TO HAVE BREAKFAST...
JIM DAVIS 11-7

AS THE SHARK APPROACHES HIS PREY, HE SENSES SOMETHING AMISS
OH, YEAH, WATER! SHARKS NEED WATER!
JPM DAVIS 11-8

GOOD MORNING, GARFIELD
JIM DAVIS
11-17
Z
© 1986 United Feature Syndicate, Inc.
I HATE MONDAY MORNING PEP TALKS
Z

AHA! GOTCHA!
IT'S TIME FOR YOUR FLEA SPRAY. NOW DON'T GIVE ME ANY TROUBLE. JUST SIT THERE
© 1988 United Feature Syndicate, Inc.
PSSSSSSS
THAT'S MY BOY
JIM DAVIS 11-18

OKAY, MOUSE! I KNOW YOU'RE BEHIND THAT BOX! COME OUT WITH YOUR HANDS UP!
© 1986 United Feature Syndicate, Inc.
JIM DAVIS 11-19

GARFIELD! WHAT ARE YOU DOING?!
SCRATCH SCRATCH SCRATCH
© 1986 United Feature Syndicate, Inc.
YOUR CHAIR HAS AN ITCH
JIM DAVIS 11-20

Z
THIS LOOKS LIKE A NICE PLACE...
Z
© 1986 United Feature Syndicate,Inc.
FOR A NAP
Z
JIM DAVIS 11-21

LOOK, GARFIELD. I GOT YOU A WATER BED!
JIM DAVIS 11-22
WATER BEDS ARE ALL THE RAGE, RIGHT? YOU ALWAYS WANTED A WATER BED, RIGHT?
RIGHT
© 1986 United Feature Syndicate, Inc.
BUT A HOT WATER BOTTLE IN A BOX?

YOU THINK TOO MUCH ABOUT FOOD, GARFIELD. YOU NEED A DISTRACTION
JIM DAVIS
TRY READING A BOOK
NOVEL IDEA
© 1986 United Feature Syndicate,Inc.
COOK BOOK
11-24

I HAVE A SPECIAL SURPRISE FOR YOU TODAY, GARFIELD!
GARFIELD
11-25
GENERIC CAT FOOD
CAT FOOD
GARFIELD
© 1988 United Feature Syndicate, Inc.
SPLAT!
THEN FEED IT TO A GENERIC CAT!
TOING
GARFIELD
JIM DAVIS

YOU KNOW, GARFIELD, YOU SHOULD REALLY BE THANKFUL FOR THE FOOD YOU EAT
GARFIELD
I AM, JON. I AM
GARFIELD
© 1986 United Feature Syndicate, Inc.
11-26
I'M ALSO THANKFUL FOR THE FOOD YOU EAT
JIM DAVIS
GARFIELD

ISN'T LIFE GREAT, GARFIELD? WE SHOULD COUNT OUR BLESSINGS
ZIP!
© 1986 United Feature Syndicate, Inc.
WHEW! THEY'RE ALL THERE!
JIM DAVIS
11-27

GARFIELD, DID YOU EAT MY JELLY FILLED DOUGHNUT?
11-28
IT WAS LIKE THIS, JON. IT HAPPENED TO BE A ROGUE DOUGHNUT WOUNDED IN A JUNGLE BAKERY
© 1986 United Feature Syndicate, Inc.
CRAZED WITH FEAR AND PAIN, IT CHARGED MY MOUTH AND I WAS FORCED TO EAT IT IN SELF-DEFENSE
IT'S TIMES LIKE THIS I WISH I UNDERSTOOD HIM
JIM DAVIS

I'M HOME!
JIM DAVIS
HI, GARFIELD
YOU'RE SO NICE TO COME HOME TO!
11-29

IF THE EARLY BIRD GETS THE WORM, THEN THE EARLY CAT SHOULD GET THE BIRD
SO I'LL JUST STEP OUTSIDE AND GET AN...
EARLY DOG!
JIM DAVIS 12-2

I THINK I'LL TAKE A SHORT NAP
HEE HEE HEE
WHOEVER HEARD OF A TALL NAP?
JIM DAVIS 12-1

YAWN
SMACK SMACK SMACK
© 1986 United Feature Syndicate, Inc.
I WISH JON WOULD WARN ME BEFORE HE TURNS THE FURNACE ON
JIM DAVIS 12-3

SOME PEOPLE LOSE WEIGHT
I JUST GIVE IT A TEMPORARY LEAVE OF ABSENCE
JIM DAVIS 12-4

DON'T EAT THIS PIE, GARFIELD
I WON'T

YOU WON'T FORGET WILL YOU?
I WON'T FORGET. I NEVER FORGET

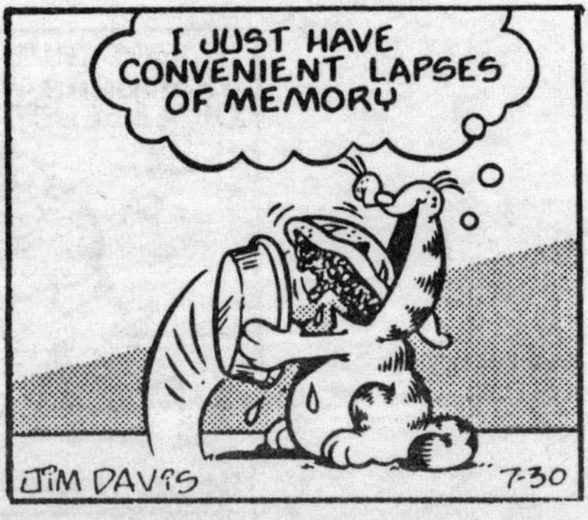
I JUST HAVE CONVENIENT LAPSES OF MEMORY
JIM DAVIS
7-30

SORRY, BOYS. I JUST RAN OUT OF COFFEE
WHAT?!
WAIT! YOU'RE IN LUCK. I JUST REMEMBERED...
© 1986 United Feature Syndicate, Inc.
THE LAST GUY IN HERE SPILLED HIS
I THINK I'M GOING TO BE SICK
JIM DAVIS 7-31

THIS IS GREAT. WHAT DID MOM USED TO SAY ABOUT SLEEPING IN LAUNDRY BASKETS?
© 1986 United Feature Syndicate, Inc.
AH, YES...."MY SON, SLEEP ONLY IN THE CLEAN LAUNDRY"
JIM DAVIS 8-1

THIS MIRROR SHOULD SHAME GARFIELD INTO LOSING SOME WEIGHT
GARFIELD
GARFIELD
WHY, THANK YOU FOR THE CHARMING AND WITTY DINNER COMPANION, JON
YOU CAN'T SHAME A SHAMELESS CAT
GARFIELD
JIM DAVIS 8-2
© 1986 United Feature Syndicate, Inc.

THERE'S NO ESCAPING IT!

IT'S GONNA GET ME!

AHCHOO!
JIM DAVIS
7-14

SNIFF. I'M ALLERGIC TO SOMETHING AROUND HERE. I WONDER IF IT'S DOGS?
SNIFF!
NOPE
JIM DAVIS
7-15

AH, AH
AH, AHH!
© 1986 United Feature Syndicate, Inc.
CHOOO!
7-16
JIM DAVIS

JIM DAVIS 7-17
SNIFF
SNIFF
SNUCK!
YES, GARFIELD. I KNOW YOU'RE NOT FEELING WELL

I'M GONNA SNEEZE! AH-AHH AHHH!
FFFT
© 1986 United Feature Syndicate, Inc.
THANK YOU. WHERE ARE YOU GOING?
I'M GOING TO BOIL MY FINGER NOW
JIM DAVIS 7-18

THIS IS WHAT'S BEEN MAKING ME SNEEZE! IT'S JON'S COLOGNE
IT'S CALLED "DITCHDIGGER, THE WORKING MAN'S COLOGNE"
© 1986 United Feature Syndicate, Inc.
JIM DAVIS 7-19
AND, AS YOU KNOW, I'M ALLERGIC TO WORK

GOOD HEAVENS! I'M GOING TO BE EIGHT YEARS OLD THIS THURSDAY!
JUNE
JIM DAVIS
6-16
I HATE BIRTHDAYS. THEY'RE A LOT LIKE CALENDARS
JUNE
THEY REMIND YOU YOUR DAYS ARE NUMBERED
JUNE

HEY! THERE'S SOMEBODY IN BED WITH ME!
JIM DAVIS
6-17
OH, IT'S YOU...
© 1986 United Feature Syndicate, Inc.
GOOD MORNING, BELLY

I HAVE SOME BAD NEWS ABOUT YOUR BIRTHDAY CAKE, GARFIELD
JIM DAVIS 6-18
IT COLLAPSED UNDER THE WEIGHT OF THE CANDLES
IS THAT AN AGE JOKE?
OH WELL, IT WOULD PROBABLY HAVE SET OFF THE SMOKE ALARM ANYWAY
TIME-OUT! UNFAIR! AGE JOKE!

HAPPY BIRTHDAY, GARFIELD! WE LOVE YOU!
JIM DAVIS 6-19
DO YOU KNOW THE BEST PART OF BIRTHDAYS?
© 1986 United Feature Syndicate, Inc.
FOR A DAY, IT'S NICE TO HAVE THE WORLD REVOLVE AROUND YOU!

HAPPY BIRTHDAY, GARFIELD. HERE'S A DOUBLE-CHOCOLATE FUDGE MARSHMALLOW CREAM CAKE!
JIM DAVIS 6-20
AND HERE'S CHOCOLATE CHIP ICE CREAM, SUGAR COOKIES AND A CHERRY PHOSPHATE! ANY QUESTIONS?
YEH...
© 1986 United Feature Syndicate, Inc.
WHAT'S FOR DESSERT?

Garfield
Le Magnifique!

JIM DAVIS

JIM DAVIS
1-26
SPLANG
© 1989 United Feature Syndicate, Inc
AH YES, THE OL' "SECONDS AWAY FROM BLISSFUL SLUMBER" BODY SPASM

POP!
1-27
POP!
POP! POP!
POP!
POP!
POP!
POP! POP! POP!
JIM DAVIS
© 1989 United Feature Syndicate, Inc.
WE'RE OUT OF POPCORN

GARFIELD, WOULD YOU SAY I HAVE AN INTERESTING PERSONALITY?
JIM DAVIS
1-28

YES, I WOULD

I'D BE LYING, BUT I'D SAY IT

WHAT A BORING LIFE I HAVE
HOW COULD ANYONE HAVE A MORE BORING LIFE?
THIS IS IT, GARFIELD!
TODAY'S THE DAY I TWEEZE MY EAR HAIRS!
I GUESS ANYTHING IS POSSIBLE
JIM DAVIS
1-30

1-31
HI, ODIE!
© 1989 United Feature Syndicate, Inc.
THUD!
THAT WAS TOO EASY
JIM DAVIS

JIM DAVIS
Z
OH
2-1

2-2
© 1989 United Feature Syndicate, Inc.
BWOING!
BREAKFAST IN BED, GARFIELD?
SLOTH IS THE MOTHER OF INVENTION
JIM DAVIS

2-3
DOGS ARE THE ANIMAL BY-PRODUCTS IN THE WEENIE OF LIFE
JIM DAVIS

JIM DAVIS 2-4
WOOAAH!
THANKS A LOT FOR WRECKING MY SHOT, MR. TWINKLE TOES!

I HATE FEBRUARY
JIM DAVIS
2-6

FEBRUARY IS THE ARMPIT OF THE YEAR

AND DON'T EVEN TALK TO ME ABOUT MONDAYS IN FEBRUARY

DEPRESSED, GARFIELD?
HOW COULD YOU TELL?
JIM DAVIS

I'M JUST A FAT DOILY ON THE EASY CHAIR OF LIFE
JIM DAVIS
KACHUCK
WHOP
CHECK THAT. ON THE "RECLINER OF LIFE"
2-8

JIM DAVIS
2-9
KA-
CHUCK

KA-
CHUCK
© 1989 United Feature Syndicate, Inc.
JIM DAVIS
2-10

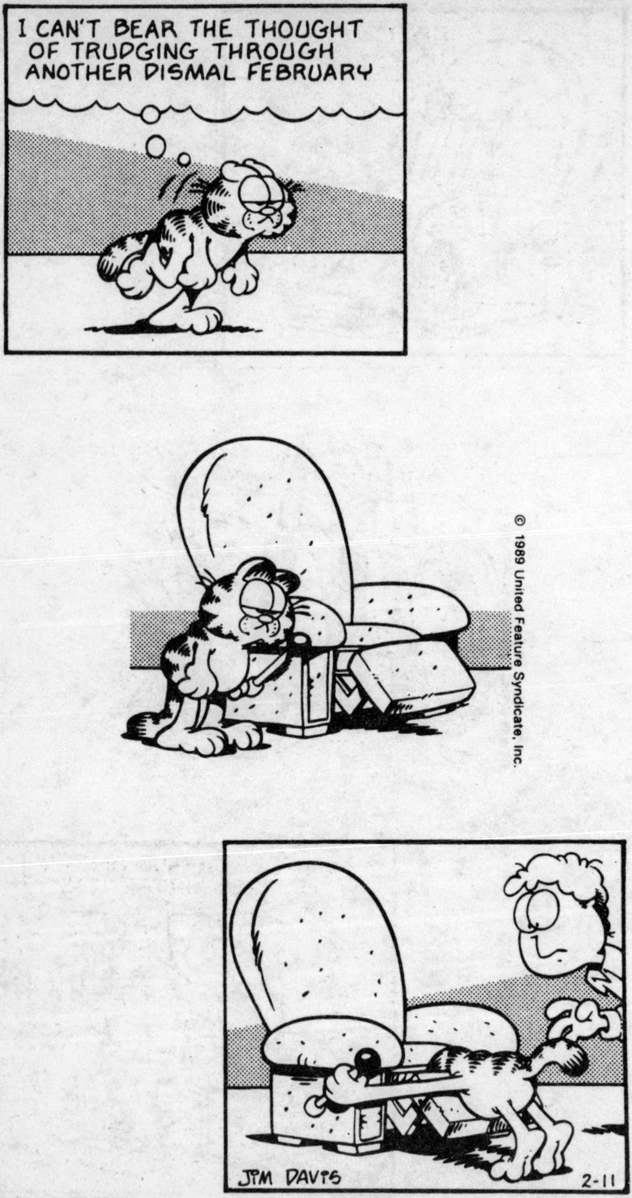
I CAN'T BEAR THE THOUGHT OF TRUDGING THROUGH ANOTHER DISMAL FEBRUARY
© 1989 United Feature Syndicate, Inc.
JIM DAVIS
2-11

WAKE UP, GARFIELD. IT'S A BEAUTIFUL FEBRUARY MORNING
WAKE ME WHEN IT'S MARCH
IT'S MONDAY, THE START OF A BRAND NEW WEEK
STRIKE TWO
FEBRUARY, MONDAY THE THIRTEENTH!
AAARGH!
JIM DAVIS
2-13

WHIRR
© 1989 United Feature Syndicate, Inc.
2-14
JIM DAVIS

THIS IS GOING TO BE ONE GOOD CUP OF COFFEE!
JIM DAVIS 2-15
© 1989 United Feature Syndicate, Inc.

GARFIELD! DINNER!
GARFIELD
© 1989 United Feature Syndicate, Inc.
GARFIELD
SPLOOT
JIM DAVIS
2-16
BOY, I GOTTA PRACTICE MY AIM!
GARFIELD

COMICS
ODIE
JIM DAVIS
2-17
COMICS
ODIE
HE'S SO IMPRESSIONABLE

GOOD MORNING, POOKY
2-18
POO!
AND JUST WHERE ARE YOU GOING WITH MY TEDDY BEAR?
UH, IT'S MY KID'S BIRTHDAY
JIM DAVIS

YO, ARLENE. HEY, BA-BEEE
LATER, DOLL FACE
AREN'T YOU GOING TO STOP AND VISIT?
© 1989 United Feature Syndicate, Inc.
I WON'T HAVE TO MAKE ANY LIKE, **REAL** CONVERSATION, WILL I?
PERISH THE THOUGHT
JIM DAVIS
2-20

I'D LOVE TO STAY AND CHAT, ARLENE, BUT I'M GOING TO THE DOG POUND TO POUND SOME DOGS
THEN, I'M GOING TO THE GYM TO PUMP SOME IRON
JIM DAVIS 2-21
© 1989 United Feature Syndicate, Inc.
YES. AND I DO BELIEVE THE GYMNASIUM IS THIS WAY
WELCOME TO AN EVENING OF MACHO POSTURING

JUST LOOK AT THAT MOON, GARFIELD
DOESN'T IT GIVE YOU ANY IDEAS?
SURE DOES...
© 1989 United Feature Syndicate, Inc.
2-22
JIM DAVIS
BARK! BARK!
SIGH

OH, GARFIELD, GARFIELD, GARFIELD, GARFIELD, GARFIELD...
GARFIELD, GARFIELD, GARFIELD, GARFIELD...
ARLENE?
© 1989 United Feature Syndicate, Inc.
2-23
JIM DAVIS
YES, GARFIELD?
SHUT UP, ARLENE

AJAX DOG WHISTLE
works every time.

MEOW
FFFFF
2-24
JIM DAVIS

GAR-FIELD! ODI-
GARFIELD
ODIE
2-25
GULP GULP
SHOOM
GARFIELD
ODIE
JIM DAVIS
© 1989 United Feature Syndicate, Inc.
FASTER THAN THE SPEED OF DOG
PAT PAT
GARFIELD
ODIE

ANYONE HERE TONIGHT FROM OUT OF TOWN?
ANYONE HERE FROM IN TOWN?
2-27
JIM DAVIS
ANYONE HERE?

I SAW THIS DOG THE OTHER DAY, AND HE SAID HE HADN'T HAD A BITE IN THREE DAYS, SOOOO...

I LET HIM BITE ME!
JIM DAVIS
2-28

ROWF!
HARF
HYUH
YARK
I GIVE 'EM WHAT THEY WANT
YARK
HYUK
HAR HAR
HAR

TAPPITY
TAPPITY
TAPPITY
TAPPITY
TAPPITY
TAPPITY

WHAT DO YOU GET WHEN YOU CROSS A DOG WITH A NINE-FOOT GORILLA?
3-1
JIM DAVIS
© 1989 United Feature Syndicate, Inc

YOU GET A GORILLA THAT DRINKS OUT OF ANY TOILET HE PLEASES!

NOW TO THE ENTERTAINMENT PORTION OF OUR SHOW
AN AMAZING FEAT OF VENTRILOQUISM
© 1989 United Feature Syndicate, Inc.
JIM DAVIS
3-2
FEATURING MY OVERQUALIFIED ASSISTANT

SAY HI TO THE PEOPLE, DUMMY
HI TO THE PEOPLE, DUMMY
© 1989 United Feature Syndicate, Inc.
3-3
JIM DAVIS
YOU'LL NOTICE MY LIPS NEVER MOVED

GLUG
GLUG
GLUG
LADEEEE OF SPAIN, I ADORE YOU
3-4
JIM DAVIS
© 1989 United Feature Syndicate, Inc.

I FEEL DOWN TODAY, GARFIELD
3-6
OH, 'DEM BLUES. DEY DONE GOT ME DOWN. OH, YEAH
SOMETIMES I JUST GOTTA LET IT OUT
I WAS HOPING WE'D HAVE TO OPERATE
JIM DAVIS

THE FLOOR IS FREEZING!
JIM DAVIS

HEY! WHERE'S MY OTHER SLIPPER?!

3-7

HOP HOP

HEY, GARFIELD, HOW ABOUT GOING FOR A RIDE?
GREAT!
I MEANT IN THE CAR
PIGGYBACK POOPER
JIM DAVIS
3-8

THIS TASTES A BIT ODD, IRMA
OOPS, WRONG DISH
JIM DAVIS 3-9
© 1989 United Feature Syndicate, Inc
HERE, FIDO!
I THINK I'LL SKIP DESSERT

I'M READY FOR MY BIG DATE, GARFIELD
WHAT THE...?
JIM DAVIS 3-10
© 1989 United Feature Syndicate, Inc.
THAT'S WHERE I HID THE BANANA CREAM PIE!

JIM DAVIS
3-11
TWEET
I ALWAYS WONDERED WHAT "TWEET" MEANT

POIT
© 1989 United Feature Syndicate, Inc.
JIM DAVIS 3-13
SNIP!
AIEEEEE

3-14
© 1989 United Feature Syndicate, Inc
WHAP!
JIM DAVIS

SO LONG, SPIDER

FLINK

GARFIELD
JIM DAVIS
3-15

© 1989 United Feature Syndicate, Inc.
JIM DAVIS
3-16

SQUISH
JIM DAVIS
3-17

WHAP!
JIM DAVIS 3-18

SOMETIMES I LIKE TO WATCH LIFE'S PASSING PARADE
AND SOMETIMES THE PARADE LIKES TO WATCH ME
JIM DAVIS 3-20

TIME TO GET UP, GARFIELD
Z
YAWN
Z
JIM DAVIS
3-21

3-22 JIM DAVIS

HEY, WAIT A MINUTE...

GARFIELD! WHAT HAPPENED!
JIM DAVIS
3-23
I YAWNED AND LOCKED MY JAW
© 1989 United Feature Syndicate, Inc.
IS THERE ANYTHING I CAN DO?
HERE, KEEP THE FLIES AWAY FROM MY MOUTH

BEAUTIFUL NIGHT, HUH, GARFIELD?
3-24
MY AUNT ORPHA USED TO TAKE LONG WALKS AT NIGHT
THAT'S NICE
© 1989 United Feature Syndicate, Inc.
TILL SHE GOT A BAT IN HER HAIR
CAN WE GO IN NOW?
JPM DAVPS

JIM DAVIS 3-25
HEY, MOUSE
KNOCK KNOCK
I DON'T MEAN TO COMPLAIN, BUT WHAT ARE YOU TRYING TO DO?
MAKE ME LOOK BAD?

GOOD MORNING GARFIELD
THERE GOES THE CRUELEST MAN ALIVE
JIM DAVIS
3-27

SHTOING!
© 1989 United Feature Syndicate, Inc
THANK GOODNESS I MISSED THE APPLE
JIM DAVIS
3-28

DO YOU KNOW WHAT'S REALLY DANGEROUS? IT'S THOSE LITTLE TOY BALLS WITH BELLS IN THEM
JIM DAVIS
3-29
OH-NO!
DINGLE
DINGLE
BOOM!

AS LONG AS I'M DOWN HERE, I MIGHT AS WELL ATTEMPT TO SIT UP
AH, YES... THE PATH OF LEAST RESISTANCE
© 1989 United Feature Syndicate, Inc
JIM DAVIS
3-30

ODIE!
© 1989 United Feature Syndicate, Inc.
JIM DAVIS
3·31
GARFIELD! PUT THOSE CYMBALS AWAY!
I CAN'T HAVE ANY FUN

TIME TO RAID THE REFRIGERATOR
JIM DAVIS 4-1
BANZAI!
I TAKE NO PRISONERS

OKAY, A DINKY LITTLE MOUSE HOLE. I HAVE NO PROBLEM WITH THAT
NOW THAT'S A PROBLEM
JIM DAVIS
4-3

JIM DAVIS 4-4
GOTCHA!
© 1989 United Feature Syndicate, Inc.
TAG! YOU'RE IT!

PSHHHHH

4-5
JIM DAVIS

SCRIBBLE
SCRIBBLE
SCRIBBLE

BOY, DID I WALK INTO THAT ONE
JIM DAVIS
4-6

UH-OH
4-7
JIM DAVIS

JON'S NOT GOING TO BE HAPPY ABOUT THIS

THEY'VE GONE CONDO

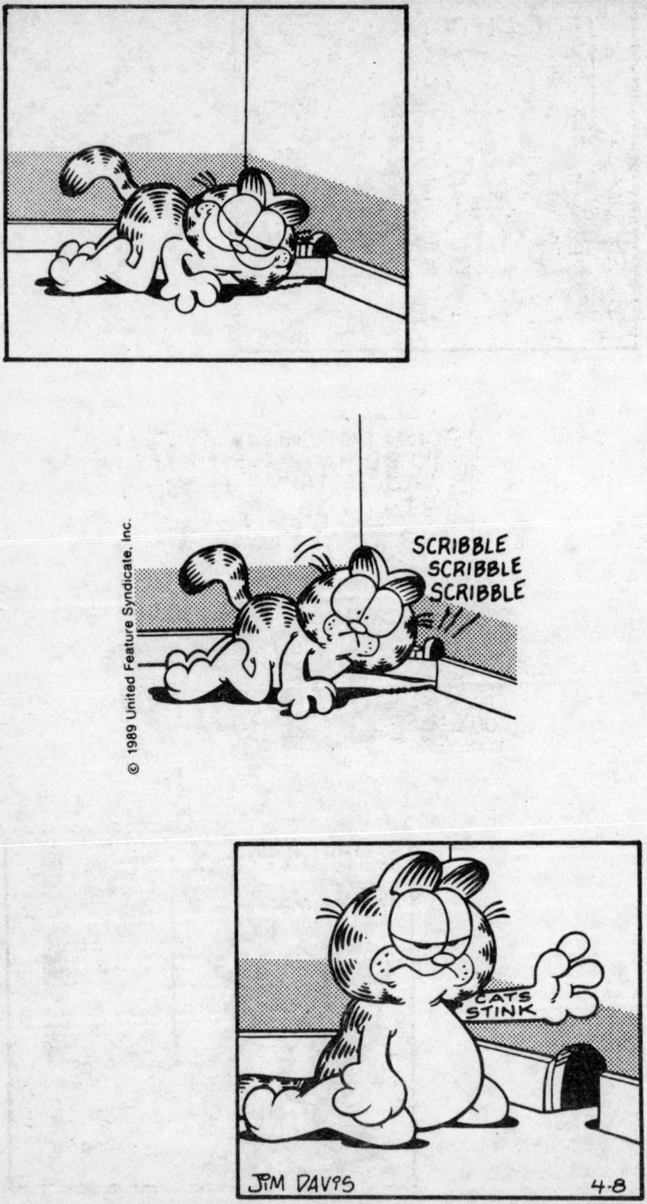
SCRIBBLE
SCRIBBLE
SCRIBBLE
CATS STINK
JIM DAVIS
4-8

JIM DAVIS

GARFIELD!
4-10

OH, SURE! BLAME ME!

GARFIELD, WHAT WOULD YOU THINK IF I BROUGHT A CANARY HOME?
4-11
© 1989 United Feature Syndicate, Inc
ZIP!
JIM DAVIS
YOU'RE DISGUSTING

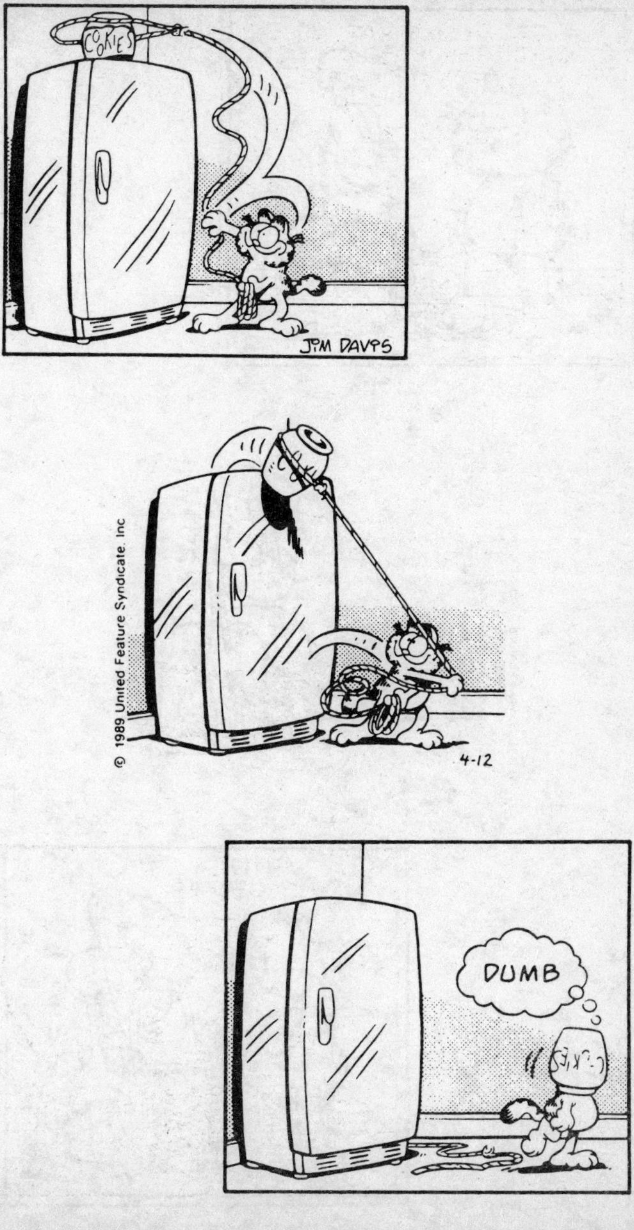
COOKIES
JIM DAVIS
© 1989 United Feature Syndicate, Inc
4-12
DUMB

4-13
JIM DAVIS

INSOMNIA IS A TERRIBLE THING
I'VE BEEN LYING HERE, WIDE AWAKE...
ALL AFTERNOON!
GET UP
JIM DAVIS
4-14

HMMMM
JIM DAVIS
SLAP! SLAP! SLAP! SLAP! SLAP! SLAP! SLAP!
4-15
GARFIELD! WHAT HAPPENED?!
JUST HOW LONG HAS THAT LEFTOVER SAUERKRAUT BEEN IN THERE?

HEY! I WAS GOING TO SIT THERE, GARFIELD
GET LOST

HEY!
GET LOST
JIM DAVIS
4-17

NOT ONLY ARE WE DULL... WE'RE WEIRD, TOO
JIM DAVIS
4-18
TONIGHT'S SPAGHETTI NIGHT
THAT'S WHEN WE SIT AROUND AND PRETEND WE'RE EATING OUR HAIR

THERE'S CRAZY UNCLE ED
JIM DAVIS
HE LIKED TO SNIFF WAFFLE IRONS
© 1989 United Feature Syndicate, Inc
WE SPENT MANY HAPPY HOURS PLAYING TIC-TAC-TOE ON HIS FACE
4-19

MILK
GOOD, GARFIELD'S NOT AROUND. I WON'T HAVE TO SHARE MY MILK
MILK
JIM DAVIS
4-20

MY DATE WAS GOING REAL WELL TONIGHT
MY SOPHISTICATION SWEPT HER OFF HER FEET
JIM DAVIS 4-21
© 1989 United Feature Syndicate, Inc.
THEN I NOTICED I WAS WEARING MY UNDERWEAR ON THE OUTSIDE OF MY PANTS
SICK

GARFIELD, YOU MADE ME BREAKFAST!
JIM DAVIS
WHAT IS IT?
I'LL GIVE YOU A HINT
MMMM...
WHAT HAS SIX LEGS AND CAN'T SWIM IN ORANGE JUICE?
4-22

HERE IT IS. THE WORLD'S GREATEST ALARM CLOCK
JIM DAVIS

IT HAS HANDS THAT GLOW IN THE DARK

AND A SNOOZE BUTTON WITH A THREE-DAY DELAY
4-24

4-25
HEY, JON
© 1989 United Feature Syndicate, Inc.
I THINK ODIE WANTS TO COME INSIDE
JIM DAVIS

JIM DAVIS
POOR ODIE. LOCKED OUTSIDE IN THE COLD. I JUST CAN'T BEAR TO SEE HIM LIKE THIS. I GOTTA DO SOMETHING
© 1989 United Feature Syndicate, Inc.
SHOONK
4-26

"AND NOW... AN EVENING WITH MOZART"

SIGH
© 1989 United Feature Syndicate, Inc.
SIGH
JIM DAVIS
4-28

CRUNCH!!!
SPOOT!
JIM DAVIS
4-29
CRUNCH
CRONCH
CRONCH
CRUNCH
CRONCH
GARFIELD! WHAT ON EARTH ARE YOU CRUNCHING ON?
YOUR COFFEE

HERE COMES ARLENE. SHE'S CRAZY ABOUT ME
5-1
JIM DAVIS
I HATE IT WHEN YOU GROVEL LIKE THAT, ARLENE!

HERE COMES ARLENE. I THINK I'LL SUCK IN MY STOMACH AND THROW OUT MY CHEST
5-2
© 1989 United Feature Syndicate, Inc.
YOU GOT IT BACKWARDS AGAIN, DUMMY
JIM DAVIS

HEY, ARLENE, BAY-BEE... WANNA SIT ON THE FENCE AND HOWL?
JIM DAVIS
BLOW IT OUT YOUR FIRE HYDRANT, BLIMPO
5-3
© 1989 United Feature Syndicate, Inc.
GOOSH!

COME UP ON THE FENCE WITH ME, ARLENE
5-4
JIM DAVIS
HOW DO I GET UP THERE?
TAKE MY HAND, LITTLE LADY
© 1989 United Feature Syndicate, Inc.
I SAID "TAKE," NOT "PULL"!

ARLENE, YOUR LIPS ARE AS RED AS TOMATO SAUCE...
JIM DAVIS
YOUR SKIN IS AS PALE AS UNCOOKED PASTA...
© 1989 United Feature Syndicate, Inc.
YOUR EYES! THEY'RE SOFT AS MOZZARELLA! YOUR HAIR!...
HEY, VALENTINO! IS THIS A DATE OR A FEEDING FRENZY?
5-5

DO YOU HAVE ANY PETS, JON?
YES. A CAT AND A DOG
REALLY? WHAT KIND OF CAT?
OH, JUST AN ORDINARY HOUSE CAT
JIM DAVIS 5-6
© 1989 United Feature Syndicate, Inc.
I JUST DROWNED THE ALARM CLOCK
OKAY, I LIED

Z
5-8
RIIINNNG!
SPLOT!
JIM DAVIS
© 1989 United Feature Syndicate, Inc.
RIIIINNNG!
HELLOOO MONDAY
RFIELD

HERE I STAND ON TOP OF THE WORLD. MASTER OF ALL I SEE
JIM DAVIS
NONE DARE CHALLENGE ME, UNLESS OF COURSE THEY BE FOOLS, OR...
5-9

YES, NERMAL, LIFE IS A COMPLICATED THING. YOU GET OUT OF IT WHAT YOU PUT INTO IT
5-10
THAT WAS PRETTY INTELLECTUAL. ANY QUESTIONS?
IS IT HARD TO TALK WITH SIX CHINS?
I HATE YOU
JIM DAVIS

GIDDYAP, YOU FLEA-BITTEN PLUG!
5-11
TO THE CORRAL, YOU WORTHLESS PIECE OF HORSEFLESH!
JIM DAVIS
STUPID PET DOOR

THIS IS MY BEDDY-BYE TIME CHECKLIST
GARFIELD

BLANKET?... CHECK.
FOOD?... CHECK.
POOKY?... CHECK.
ALARM CLOCK?...
GARFIELD

CHECK
GARFIELD
5-12

CLOMP!
CLOMP!
CLOMP!
JIM DAVIS
5-13

CLOMP!
CLOMP!
CLOMP!
CLOMP!

CLOMP!

YOU GOTTA GO ON A DIET, GARFIELD
5-15
EVEN YOUR FACE IS GETTING FAT
WHOSE FACE IS FAT?!
GARFIELD
JIM DAVIS

AH, THAT WAS A NICE MEAL
JIM DAVIS

CRUMBS!
5-16

IT'S DIET WEEK
SLUP
SLUP
SLUP
SLUP

I KNOW IT'S NATURAL TO CLEAN UP YOUR DISH WHEN YOU'RE ON A DIET...
SLURP SLURP SLURP
GARFIELD
5-17
BUT, IF YOU'RE NOT CAREFUL, YOU'LL LICK A HOLE RIGHT THROUGH THAT BOWL!
GARFIELD
JIM DAVIS
GUESS AGAIN, SUCKER
GARFIELD

GLUP GLUP
JIM DAVIS
5-18
OH NO! I'VE BEEN ON THIS DIET TOO LONG!
© 1989 United Feature Syndicate, Inc
I'VE FORGOTTEN HOW TO SWALLOW!

DIET GOTCHA DOWN, GARFIELD?
I'M LOWER THAN A SNAKE'S BELLY IN A WAGON RUT
JIM DAVIS
5-19
I HAVE ABOUT AS MUCH CHANCE OF SURVIVING THIS DIET AS A ONE-LEGGED OPOSSUM ON A FREEWAY
WHY, SOON, YOU'LL BE SKINNIER THAN A STRING BEAN IN A PUMPKIN PATCH
THAT'S THE STUPIDEST THING I'VE EVER HEARD

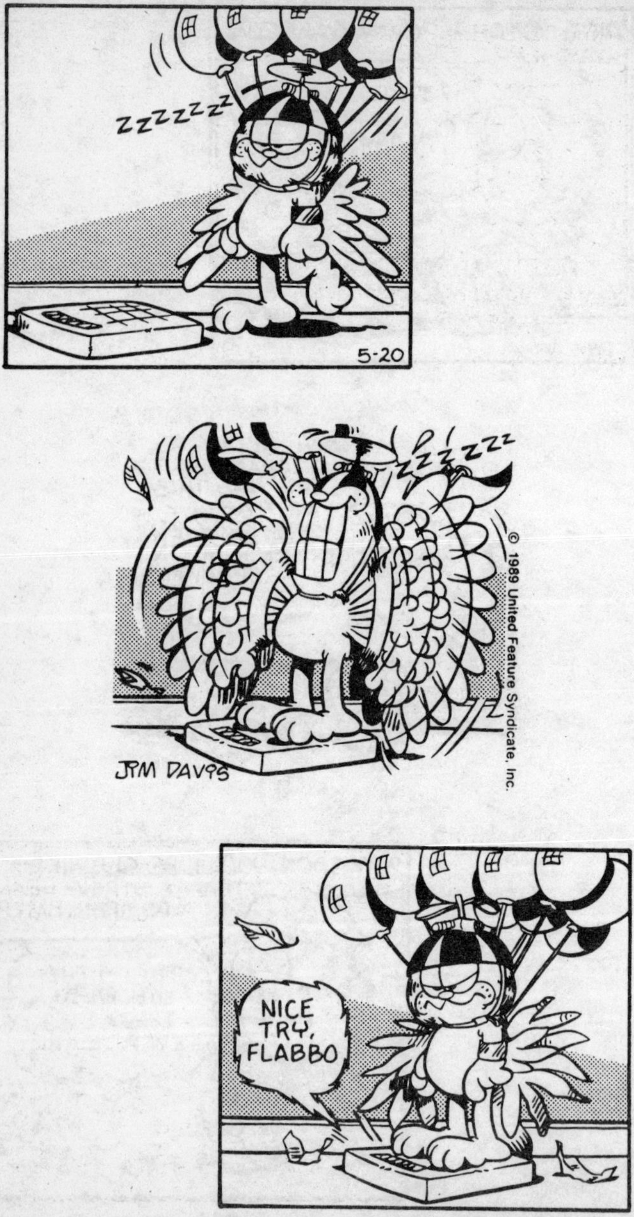
ZZZZZZZ
5-20
ZZZZZZZ
JIM DAVIS
© 1989 United Feature Syndicate, Inc.
NICE TRY, FLABBO

TRY THIS NEW CAT FOOD, GARFIELD
NO THANKS
GARFIELD
JIM DAVIS
5-22

IT HAS BEEF, LIVER, CHICKEN...
NOT INTERESTED
GARFIELD

LEG OF MAILMAN
YOU WOULDN'T KID ABOUT THAT, WOULD YOU?
GARFIELD

I HATE IT WHEN MUD BUILDS UP ON MY FEET
KNOCK
KNOCK
KNOCK
© 1989 United Feature Syndicate, Inc.
YAAAH!
JIM DAVIS
5-23

UP AND AT 'EM, GARFIELD!
THERE'S A BIG, WIDE, WONDERFUL WORLD OUT THERE!
TRUE...
BUT, THERE'S A SMALL, SOFT, WARM BED IN HERE
JIM DAVIS
5-24

5-25
TAP
TAP
© 1989 United Feature Syndicate, Inc.
JIM DAVIS

ODIE LEFT HIS BRAIN TO SCIENCE
5-26
© 1989 United Feature Syndicate, Inc.
AND THEY MADE AN EARLY WITHDRAWAL
JIM DAVIS

Z
Z
JIM DAVIS
5-27

I'M EXHAUSTED!
I GUESS I OVERDID IT
THAT'S THE LAST TIME I TAKE THREE NAPS IN A ROW WITHOUT A BREAK
JIM DAVIS
5-29

HELLO? DEBBIE, MY SWEET?
YOU FAT GREEDY PIG! I OUGHTA SHAVE YOU BALD AND PUT YOU OUT IN THE COLD
© 1989 United Feature Syndicate, Inc.
5-30
HELLO?
CLICK
JIM DAVIS

DO YOU THINK THIS TIE IS TOO WIDE, GARFIELD?
ABSOLUTELY NOT
JIM DAVIS 5-31
HOWEVER, YOU DO NEED TO GAIN ABOUT 300 POUNDS

I'M LOOKING FOR JUST THE RIGHT COLOGNE
THAT, COUPLED WITH MY PERSONALITY, WILL RENDER WOMEN HELPLESS
© 1989 United Feature Syndicate, Inc
JIM DAVIS 6-1
MAYBE YOU SHOULD TRY CHLOROFORM

6-2
JIM DAVIS
MY DATE AND I WENT HIKING
WE DRANK FRESH WATER FROM A STREAM
I GOT A LEECH ON MY FOREHEAD
LOTS OF SCREAMING, I HOPE

AREN'T YOU EVER GOING TO GET UP TODAY, GARFIELD?!
JON, JON, JON...
YOU DON'T UNDERSTAND. SLEEPING IS AN ART...
SO LET'S NOT BE DISTURBING THE CREATIVE PROCESS, HMMMM?
JIM DAVIS
6-3

THERE'S ONE THING I LIKE ABOUT LIVING HERE...
GARFIELD
SPLUT!
GARFIELD
JIM DAVIS
6-5
THE EASY COMMUTE
GARFIELD

WHEW
BANZAI!
YAAAH!
JIM DAVIS
6-6

GARFIELD
JIM DAVIS 6-7
© 1989 United Feature Syndicate, Inc.
WHAT'S THE IDEA OF PUTTING GLOP IN MY WASHING MACHINE?!
WHAT'S THE IDEA OF PUTTING DIRTY LAUNDRY IN MY INSTANT PUDDING?!

"BOING" "BOING" "BOING" "BOING"
I WONDER WHERE GARFIELD GOT THE SPRINGS
OH
JIM DAVIS
6-8

RATS! THE CHANNEL WON'T TURN
THE TV'S BROKEN, GARFIELD
CLICK CLICK CLICK CLICK
HERE, READ A BOOK FOR A CHANGE
RATS! THE PAGES WON'T TURN!
CLICK CLICK CLICK
JIM DAVIS 6-9

BREAKFAST, GARFIELD!
Z
GARFIE
THUD!
© 1989 United Feature Syndicate, Inc.
JIM DAVIS 6-10
ISN'T THAT SAD?
Z
GARFIELD

GROWING OLD IS SAD, GARFIELD
© 1989 United Feature Syndicate, Inc.
SO MANY DREAMS NEVER TO BE FULFILLED...
I MAY NEVER PLAY THE BAGPIPES!
STOP. YOU'RE RIPPING MY HEART OUT
JIM DAVIS
6-12

LISTEN TO THIS, GARFIELD
AS WE GROW OLDER, OUR ATTENTION SPAN GETS SHORTER
PRETTY INTERESTING, HUH?
WHAT?
JIM DAVIS 6-13
© 1989 United Feature Syndicate, Inc.

NEXT WEEK I'M GOING TO TURN ELEVEN
GARFIELD
I WONDER IF I'LL BE OLDER AND WISER
ARFIELD
6-14
PROBABLY JUST OLDER
ARFIELD
JIM DAVIS

HEY, GARFIELD! WHERE ARE YOU?
OH, JUST LYING HERE IN THE CORNER, THINKING ABOUT MY BIRTHDAY AND COUNTING MY WRINKLES
6-15
THE ONLY THING THAT CAN CHEER ME UP IS TO HAVE A REALLY GREAT BIRTHDAY PARTY... WITH ALL MY BEST FRIENDS
AND **YOU'RE** NOT INVITED!
JIM DAVIS

TLING
JIM DAVIS
© 1989 United Feature Syndicate, Inc.
TLING
TLING TLING
TLING
TLING
TLING
TLING
6-16
LOOKING FOR YOUR BIRTHDAY GIFT IN THE CLOSET?
OH, SHUT UP

HEY, JON...
JIM DAVIS
6-17
I KNOW I SAID I WANTED A "BIG" BIRTHDAY PARTY...
BUT, THIS IS RIDICULOUS

Garfield
Plays It Again

JIM DAVIS

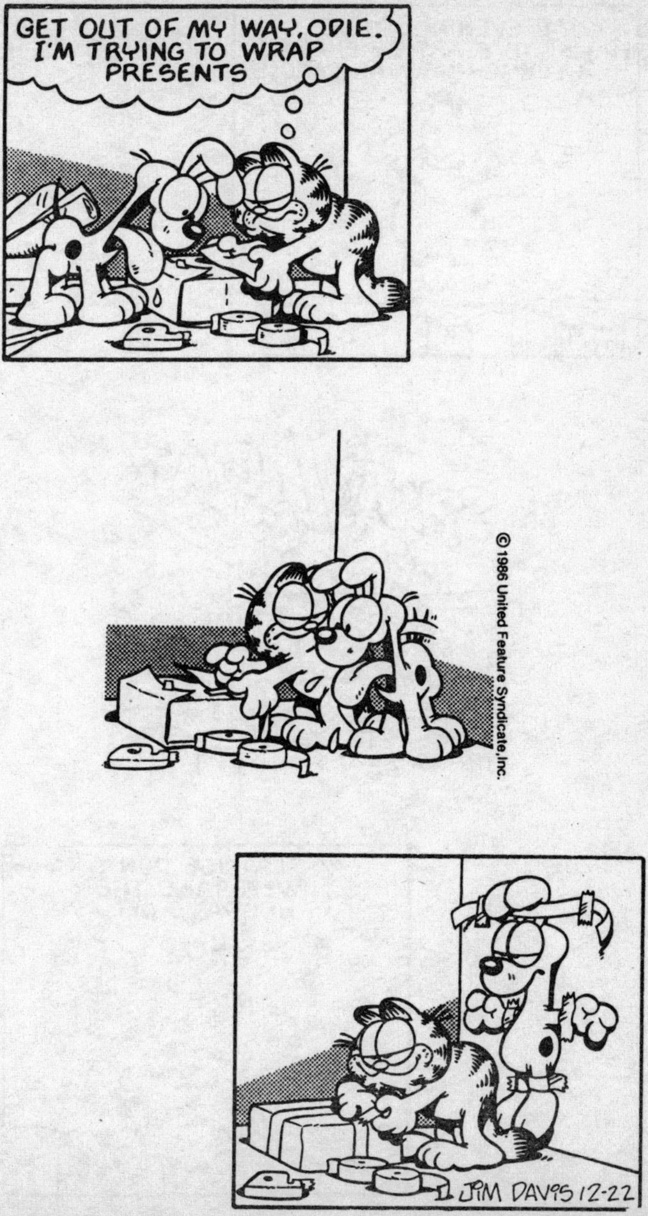
GET OUT OF MY WAY, ODIE. I'M TRYING TO WRAP PRESENTS
JIM DAVIS 12-22

GOOD EVENING, FOLKS. I'D LIKE TO START BY SINGING A FEW CHRISTMAS CAROLS!
SPLUT!
BLAT!
SPLAT!
JIM DAVIS 12-23
© 1986 United Feature Syndicate, Inc.
CRITICS DON'T EVEN TAKE THE HOLIDAYS OFF

WELL, THE GIFTS ARE UNDER THE TREE AND THE FOOD IS PREPARED. THERE'S ONLY ONE MORE ORDER OF BUSINESS...
I JUST WANT TO TELL YOU GUYS HOW MUCH I LOVE YOU
JIM DAVIS
JON IS LIKE CHRISTMAS. I ONLY APPRECIATE HIM ONCE A YEAR
12-24

JIM DAVIS 12-25
WAKE UP, BOYS! IT'S CHRISTMAS MORNING!
LET'S SEE IF SANTA BROUGHT GIFTS FOR ALL THE GOOD LITTLE CHILDREN
I GUESS NOT. HERE'S ONE FOR GARFIELD
WHAT THE HECK, IT'S CHRISTMAS. I'LL LET HIM LIVE

THE DAY AFTER CHRISTMAS I ALWAYS GET DEPRESSED
DO YOU KNOW WHAT I MEAN, GARFIELD?
YES, I DO
© 1986 United Feature Syndicate, Inc.
IF I WERE YOU I'D BE DEPRESSED EVERY DAY
JIM DAVIS
12-26

WHAT A DIPPY SWEATER
IT'S NOT THE GIFT, BUT THE THOUGHT THAT COUNTS
© 1986 United Feature Syndicate, Inc.
JIM DAVIS 12-27
OKAY, OKAY, I **THINK** IT'S A DIPPY SWEATER

GOOD MORNING, POOKY
JIM DAVIS
12-15
TEDDY BEARS ARE GREAT TO SLEEP WITH
© 1986 United Feature Syndicate, Inc.
NO MORNING BREATH

SQUEEZE
© 1986 United Feature Syndicate, Inc.
JIM DAVIS 12-16

HA, HA, HA! YOU SQUEEZED POOKY TOO HARD HUH? THAT'S HYSTERICAL!
SQUEEZE
© 1986 United Feature Syndicate, Inc.
JIM DAVIS 12-17

JIM DAVIS 12-18
SQUEEZE
ARRRGH!

GOOD NEWS, GARFIELD
I COMPLETELY RESTUFFED POOKY FOR YOU
© 1986 United Feature Syndicate, Inc.
JIM DAVIS 12-19

YOU KNOW, WITH POOKY OVERSTUFFED LIKE THAT, YOU TWO MAKE A GOOD MATCH
LIKE FATHER, LIKE SON, EH?
JIM DAVIS 12-20

CAT HAIRS!
THEY'RE A FACT OF LIFE
12-29
THERE ARE CAT HAIRS ALL OVER THE PLACE!
SO, WHAT ARE YOU GOING TO DO ABOUT IT?
I'LL BE PACKING MY BAGS AND LEAVING NOW
JIM DAVIS

WHEREVER I STOP, WE'RE STUCK WITH IT. RIGHT, GARFIELD?
RIGHT
JIM DAVIS

THE THINGS JON WILL DO FOR EXCITEMENT...
12-30

CLICK CLICK CLICK CLICK
TELEVISION ROULETTE

YOU GUYS WILL NEVER GUESS WHAT I FOUND AT THE STORE
JIM DAVIS 12-31

PHONY PET TEETH!

HAR! HAR! HAR! HAR!
LET'S BITE HIM IN THE NECK

IT'S TIME TO CLEAN THE FRIDGE, GARFIELD
I'LL CALL A S.W.A.T. TEAM
GRIM
JIM DAVIS 1-1-87
© 1986 United Feature Syndicate, Inc.
I HAVEN'T SEEN THESE OLIVES IN YEARS
AND IT'S ONLY HALFWAY BACK

YOU'RE A VERY BRAVE CAT, GARFIELD, AND I KNOW YOU WANT ME TO BE PROUD OF YOU
JIM DAVIS
1-2-87
© 1986 United Feature Syndicate, Inc.
ZOOM!
HE CAN SMELL A VISIT TO THE VET A MILE AWAY

POOKY!
JIM DAVIS 1-3-87
HOW DARE YOU HARM MY TEDDY BEAR!
POP
BAP BAP BAP
BAP BAP

ATTENTION, LOUNGE LIZARDS! THIS IS YOUR WEEK IN THE SUN. TODAY WE BEGIN CELEBRATING "NATIONAL LAZY WEEK"!
WHAT'S SO GREAT ABOUT BEING LAZY, YOU SAY?
© 1986 United Feature Syndicate, Inc.
WHAT IF WAR WERE DECLARED AND NOBODY SHOWED?
JIM DAVIS 1-5-87

IS NATIONAL LAZY WEEK FOR YOU? ASK YOURSELF THIS:
WOULD YOU BE WILLING TO LEAD A PARADE IN CELEBRATION OF THE LAZY LIFE?
IF THE ANSWER IS YES... YOU'RE ALL WRONG FOR LAZY WEEK
JIM DAVIS 1-6-87

NEVER CONFUSE BEING LAZY WITH BEING APATHETIC. WE LAZY PEOPLE ARE NOT APATHETIC
APATHETIC PEOPLE DON'T CARE ABOUT ANYTHING
LAZY PEOPLE CARE. WE JUST DON'T DO ANYTHING ABOUT IT
JIM DAVIS 1-7-87

DO PEOPLE CALL YOU "WORTHLESS"? DO PEOPLE CALL YOU A "COUCH POTATO"?
JIM DAVIS 1-8-87
WHY SHOULD WE BE HELD UP TO PUBLIC RIDICULE JUST BECAUSE WE SUBSCRIBE TO A KINETICALLY PASSIVE LIFE-STYLE. WE SHOULD STAND UP FOR OURSELVES!
© 1986 United Feature Syndicate, Inc.
THE NEXT TIME PEOPLE CALL YOU LAZY, TELL 'EM YOU WERE SICK WHEN YOU WERE A KID!

DON'T FORGET THE NATIONAL LAZY WEEK MOTTO, LAZY PEOPLE. "THERE MUST BE AN EASIER WAY"
MANY GREAT IDEAS HAVE BEEN SPAWNED FROM THAT NOBLE SENTIMENT
© 1986 United Feature Syndicate, Inc.
YOU CAN BET IT WASN'T AN EXERCISE FREAK WHO INVENTED POWER STEERING
JIM DAVIS 1-9-87

FOR THOSE OF YOU WHO WANT TO STOP ABUSING YOUR BODIES THROUGH FANATIC EXERCISE, BUT CAN'T MUSTER THE WILLPOWER...
JIM DAVIS
YOU CAN NOW JOIN "GARFIELD'S EXERCISERS ANONYMOUS"
© 1986 United Feature Syndicate, Inc.
EVERY TIME YOU FEEL AN UNCONTROLLABLE URGE TO JOG, I SEND SOMEONE OVER WITH A MUG OF WARM MILK AND A TAPE OF THE BEVERLY HILLBILLIES
1-10-87

JUST AS I·SUSPECTED

JUST WHAT IS AN HEIRLOOM?
JIM DAVIS 1-16
AN HEIRLOOM IS SOMETHING THAT'S BEEN IN YOUR FAMILY FOR GENERATIONS...
© 1987 United Feature Syndicate, Inc
THAT NO ONE'S HAD THE GUTS TO PITCH OUT

JIM DAVIS 1-15

CHOMP!

SPRONG!

AH, MY DEAR, YOU'RE AS LOVELY AS EVER. BUT, YOU LOOK SO STIFF AND FORMAL IN THAT OUTFIT

WHY DON'T YOU SLIP INTO SOMETHING MORE COMFORTABLE?

LIKE ME!
JIM DAVIS 1-14

ACTUALLY, GARFIELD IS PRETTY EASY TO CARE FOR
JIM DAVIS 1-13
CATS ARE SO CLEAN, ALWAYS PRIMPING AND WASHING THEMSELVES
WE'RE OUT OF FOOT POWDER
ALMOST TO A FAULT

ISN'T THIS GREAT, GARFIELD? WE HAVE A WHOLE DAY OF FISHING AHEAD OF US!
HOTCHA

HEY! WHERE'S THE BAIT?
BAIT?
© 1987 United Feature Syndicate, Inc

GARFIELD!
I THOUGHT IT WAS SUSHI
JIM DAVIS

GARFIELD! WAKE UP!
JIM DAVIS 1-19
I'VE MADE A DECISION THAT COULD ALTER THE COURSE OF MY ENTIRE LIFE
I HAVE DECIDED TO GROW A MUSTACHE
I SUPPOSE I COULD BLAME THIS ON MONDAY

NOTICE ANYTHING DIFFERENT ABOUT ME, GARFIELD?
YOU'RE NOT DRINKING OUT OF YOUR BINKY THE CLOWN MUG
JIM DAVIS 1-20
I THINK MY MUSTACHE IS COMING IN RATHER NICELY
THAT'S NOT YOUR COCOA?
WANNA TOUCH IT? IT FEELS REALLY WEIRD
HEY, BUDDY, I HAVE TO EAT WITH THESE HANDS!

LOOK, ODIE! A HIDEOUS HAIRY MONSTER IS NESTING UNDER JON'S NOSE!
JIM DAVIS 1-21

MAYBE IT'LL SPREAD AND COVER THE REST OF HIS FACE

ARE YOU MAKING FUN OF ME?
IT MOVED!

MUSTACHES DO STRANGE THINGS TO PEOPLE
1-22
JIM DAVIS

THEY MAKE SOME GUYS THINK THEY'RE SOMEONE THEY'RE NOT

FRANKLY, MY DEAR, I DON'T GIVE A DARN
I DON'T FEEL SAFE HERE ANYMORE

ARRRGH!
JIM DAVIS 1-23

JON! WHAT HAPPENED?
I'M FINE! GO AWAY!

ARE YOU OKAY? TELL ME!
THE SHAVER SNAGGED MY MUSTACHE, OKAY?

I SHAVED MY MUSTACHE OFF, GARFIELD
DO TELL
JIM DAVIS 1·24
I DECIDED IT MADE ME LOOK LIKE A WALRUS
I'M PROUD OF YOU, JON
IT TAKES A BIG WALRUS TO ADMIT HIS MISTAKES

JIM DAVIS 1-31
STOP RIGHT THERE!
SOMETIMES THAT'S ALL A CAT UNDERSTANDS

BANG! BANG!
HELLO? ANYBODY HOME?
BRINNNNNG!
NEXT TIME, USE THE DOOR KNOCKER
SORRY
JIM DAVIS 1-30

I EAT TOO MUCH BECAUSE I'M DEPRESSED, AND I'M DEPRESSED BECAUSE I EAT TOO MUCH
GARFIELD

IT'S A VICIOUS CIRCLE...
GARFIELD

THAT TOOK YEARS TO PERFECT!
JIM DAVIS 1·29

HERE I AM FALLING ASLEEP FACE DOWN IN A BOWL OF FOOD
GA FI
THIS IS IT. I'VE REACHED THE PINNACLE OF LAZINESS AND GLUTTONY... HOW DEPRESSING
GA FI
THERE'S NO PLACE TO GO AFTER YOU'VE REACHED THE TOP
GA
JIM DAVIS 1-28

JIM DAVIS 1·27
© 1987 United Feature Syndicate, Inc.

AMUSED, GARFIELD?
THAT'S "MR. FIG FACE" TO YOU
JIM DAVIS 1-26

JIM DAVIS 2-2
BONK!
© 1987 United Feature Syndicate, Inc.
GARFIELD! SPEAK TO ME!
AUNTY EM? IS THAT YOU?

JIM DAVIS 2-3
GARFIELD! THAT WAS A NASTY FALL YOU TOOK. ARE YOU ALL RIGHT?
GARFIELD? WHO'S GARFIELD?
© 1987 United Feature Syndicate, Inc.
OH, NO! HE'S LOST HIS MEMORY!
I DO SEEM TO REMEMBER BEING HUNGRY

HAVING AMNESIA ISN'T SO BAD. IT'LL BE KIND OF FUN FINDING OUT WHAT A GREAT GUY I AM
JIM DAVIS 2-4

ARRRGH!

OH, NO! I'M A CAT!

MAYBE SEEING ODIE WILL JOG YOUR MEMORY
WHAT A SWELL LOOKING DOG. PUT 'ER THERE
YIP! YIP! YIP!
© 1987 United Feature Syndicate, Inc.
I WONDER IF I'M GOING TO LIKE THIS GARFIELD?
JPM DAVPS 2-5

LOOK, GARFIELD. IT'S POOKY! YOUR FAVORITE POSSESSION AND CLOSEST FRIEND. DO YOU REMEMBER POOKY?
JIM DAVIS 2-6
DON'T BE SILLY. I'M A GROWN CAT. WHAT WOULD I NEED WITH A TEDDY BEAR?
© 1987 United Feature Syndicate, Inc.

AMNESIA HAS WIPED MY SLATE CLEAN. I START ESTABLISHING WHO I AM TODAY
JIM DAVIS 2-7

I AM (BURP) A GLUTTON

AMNESIA IS WEIRD. THIS GARFIELD IS LIKE A TOTAL STRANGER TO ME
I KNOW NOTHING ABOUT HIM
ASIDE FROM WHAT THE CREEP DID TO MY BODY
JIM DAVIS 2·9

THIS SHOULD JOG YOUR MEMORY, GARFIELD... LASAGNA!
NO THANK YOU. YOU WOULDN'T HAVE A PLUMP, JUICY MOUSE, WOULD YOU?
© 1987 United Feature Syndicate, Inc.
ARRRGH!
I'D NEVER GET THIS STUFF OUT OF MY WHISKERS
JIM DAVIS 2-10

YOU JUST HAVE TO RESTORE GARFIELD'S MEMORY, DOC

HE DOESN'T BEAT UP ON ODIE. HE DOESN'T CLAW THE FURNITURE. HE'S NOT LAZY AND OBNOXIOUS...
LIZ
JIM DAVIS

ARE YOU SURE YOU WANT ME TO DO THIS?
COME TO THINK OF IT...
LIZ
2-11

JPM DAVPS 2·12
LET'S TEST HIS REFLEXES
DONK!
© 1987 United Feature Syndicate, Inc.
DOING!
NORMAL
FOR GARFIELD

PERHAPS GARFIELD'S AMNESIA COULD BE CURED BY LIGHTLY TRAUMATIZING HIS CRANIUM

KNOCK MY CAT ON THE HEAD ?! WHO WOULD EVER DO SUCH A THING ?!!

MAY I BE OF ASSISTANCE ?
YOU STAY OUT OF THIS
JIM DAVIS 2-13

GO AHEAD. A LITTLE TAP ON THE HEAD MAY BRING YOUR CAT'S MEMORY BACK
DONK!

GONK!
JIM DAVIS

HEY! I CAN REMEMBER! IT'S ME! GARFIELD THE CAT!
GARFIELD? WHO'S GARFIELD?
2-14

RIIINNNGG
Z
JIM DAVIS 2-16

SMASH!

I HATE ALARM CLOCKS

I HATE SPIDERS!
JIM DAVIS 2-17
© 1987 United Feature Syndicate, Inc.

STOMP!

I HATE HATING SPIDERS

JIM DAVIS 2-18
© 1987 United Feature Syndicate, Inc.
I HATE WAX DOUGHNUTS

JIM DAVIS 2-19
FWANG!
© 1987 United Feature Syndicate, Inc.
I HATE FOLDING CHAIRS

SWOOSH
BLAT!
I HATE WINDY DAYS
JIM DAVIS 2-20

Z
CRACK
© 1987 United Feature Syndicate, Inc.
I HATE LEG CRAMPS
JIM DAVIS 2·21

JIM DAVIS 2-23
© 1987 United Feature Syndicate, Inc.
GOINK
GOINK
GOINK

JIM DAVIS 2·24

MUNCH
MUNCH
MUNCH

PTOOEY

AW, POOR DOUGHNUT, YOU LOOK LONELY
JIM DAVIS 2·25
YOU NEED A FRIEND
I HAVE A LASAGNA I'D LIKE YOU TO MEET

CAN I HAVE HALF OF THAT DOUGHNUT, GARFIELD?
NO!
GOOMP!
© 1987 United Feature Syndicate, Inc.
JIM DAVIS 2-26

GARFIELD!
THAT'S MY LAST JELLY FILLED DOUGHNUT!
CLAP
SQUIP!
JIM DAVIS 2·27

WHAT FILLING MIGHT YOU BE? JELLY? CREAM?
JIM DAVIS 2-28

YOU WOULDN'T, PERCHANCE, KNOW ANYTHING ABOUT SPINACH-FILLED DOUGHNUTS, WOULD YOU?

I LOVE IT WHEN JON BAKES A CAKE
JIM DAVIS 3-7
'CAUSE I GET TO LICK THE ICING OUT OF THE BOWL
GARFIELD!!
OF COURSE, HE'D PREFER I WAIT TILL **AFTER** HE'S ICED THE CAKE

YAWN
ARRRRGH!
JIM DAVIS 3-6

ARLENE, I THINK IT'S TIME WE GET SERIOUS
YOU DO?
JIM DAVIS
YES, SERIOUS ABOUT GETTING THAT GAP BETWEEN YOUR TEETH FIXED
THE TRUTH HURTS
3-5

GARFIELD, I JUST DON'T KNOW WHAT I SEE IN YOU
IT IS A BIT OVERWHELMING, ISN'T IT?
3-4

YOU'RE RUDE, OBNOXIOUS, FAT, SELFISH, EGOTISTICAL, AND TOTALLY DEVOID OF ANY CHARM
© 1987 United Feature Syndicate, Inc.

I AM NOT EGOTISTICAL
JIM DAVIS

ARRRGH!
© 1987 United Feature Syndicate, Inc.
JIM DAVIS
IT WAS ONLY A DREAM!
IT WAS ONLY A DREAM!
IT WAS ONLY A DREAM!
3-3

WOOF!
JIM DAVIS 3-2

BACK OFF, YOU DUMB MUTT, OR I'LL SCRATCH YOUR...

ANKLES OFF

GARFIELD, YOU NEED MORE VEGETABLES IN YOUR SYSTEM
WHAT ARE YOU GOING TO DO? DRIVE A CARROT THROUGH MY HEART?
JIM DAVIS

HERE, HAVE SOME SPINACH
OH-NO!

GASP! CHOKE! COUGH!
STOP BEING SO MELODRAMATIC, GARFIELD
3-9

EAT YOUR SPINACH, GARFIELD
3-10
IT'S GOOD FOR YOU
WELL, NOW THAT'S MORE LIKE IT!
JIM DAVIS

HAVE SOME SPINACH, GARFIELD
JIM DAVIS 3-11

SURE, AND LET'S GARNISH IT WITH A BIG BOX OF RAISINS

I HATE THEM TOO!
ZIP!

SPINACH
JIM DAVIS 3-12
IT TASTES BAD.
IT LOOKS BAD
© 1987 United Feature Syndicate, Inc.
SPLUT!
IT EVEN
SOUNDS
BAD

YUCK! SPINACH!
S
3-13
JIM DAVIS
S
GARFIELD! YOU ATE ALL YOUR SPINACH!
NOT REALLY. IT'S IN THE SALTSHAKER
S

I HATE SPINACH
JIM DAVIS 3-14
IT'S GREEN, IT'S SLIMY
AND IT LOOKS LIKE IT'S MOVING

RRINNGG!
HELLO? UH, I THINK YOU HAVE THE WRONG NUMBER
JIM DAVIS 3-16
© 1987 United Feature Syndicate, Inc.
BUT... WOULD YOU CARE TO MAKE IT THE RIGHT NUMBER, SONGBIRD?
THIS IS A LONELY MAN HERE

SO WHAT'S YOUR NAME, SWEET THING?
I CAN'T BELIEVE JON!

HOW ABOUT A DATE?
TRYING TO GET A DATE WITH A WRONG NUMBER
JIM DAVIS

TOMORROW AT SEVEN? GREAT!
A DESPERATE WRONG NUMBER
3-17

GARFIELD, I'D LIKE YOU TO MEET MY DATE
JIM DAVIS 3-18
MOMMA MIA!
© 1987 United Feature Syndicate, Inc.
WHAT'S WITH YOUR CAT?
HE'S, UH, TERRIFIED OF DAISIES

NOW, BE NICE TO MY DATE. SHE MIGHT BE SENSITIVE ABOUT HER WEIGHT
HOW'D SHE GET IN HERE? THROUGH THE GARAGE DOOR?

HER NAME IS BERTHA
FIGURES
JIM DAVIS 3-19

SHE'S A LOVELY PERSON. YOU CAN'T JUDGE A BOOK BY ITS COVER, YOU KNOW
AND YOU CAN'T JUDGE A SHIP BY ITS HULL

JIM DAVIS
BERTHA, I'D LIKE YOU TO MEET GARFIELD

HE COULD USE SOME MEAT ON HIS BONES

AFFECTIONATE SORT, ISN'T HE?
HE'S A SUCKER FOR SWEET TALK
3-20

THINK, JON, THINK. THERE'S GOTTA BE **SOMETHING** NICE TO SAY TO YOUR DATE
MY, YOUR TEETH ARE ROUND
I EAT A LOT
© 1987 United Feature Syndicate, Inc.
JIM DAVIS 3-21
YOU DON'T SAY!
NO! REALLY!

NOW DON'T MAKE A BAD IMPRESSION ON MY DATE
DON'T WORRY, JON. I'LL LEAVE THAT UP TO YOU
JIM DAVIS 3-23

READY FOR DINNER, BERTHA?

IS THE SKY BLUE?
DO CATS HATE DOGS?

I THINK YOU'RE GOING TO LIKE THIS RESTAURANT, BERTHA
AS LONG AS THEY SERVE FOOD
A WOMAN AFTER MY OWN HEART
JIM DAVIS

WOULD YOU LIKE A TABLE OR A BOOTH?
A TABLE, PLEASE
AND THE LADY WILL HAVE A BOOTH
© 1987 United Feature Syndicate, Inc.

WHAT DO YOU HAVE TO DO TO GET ANY SERVICE AROUND HERE?
YOU HAVE TO GET TO YOUR TABLE FIRST
THAT'S A STUPID RULE
3-24

AND HOW WOULD MADAME LIKE HER STEAK?
JIM DAVIS

JUST RUN THE STEER BY THE TABLE AND I'LL GRAB OFF A HUNK!
© 1987 United Feature Syndicate, Inc.
3-25

HAW! HAW! HAW!
HAW! HAW! HAW!
ET TU, GARFIELD?

BOY, I COULDN'T EAT ANOTHER BITE. WOULD ONE OF YOU LIKE MY...
SHOOP!
JIM DAVIS 3-26
© 1987 United Feature Syndicate, Inc.
RRRR
RRRR
I GUESS WE WON'T NEED A DOGGIE BAG

HOW WAS YOUR MEAL, BERTHA?
GREAT!
THANKS!
SLAP!
SPLUT!
JUST BE THANKFUL SHE DIDN'T HATE IT
JIM DAVIS 3-27

IT WAS NICE MEETING YOU, BERTHA. I HOPE YOU HAD A GOOD TIME
OH, I HAD A WONDERFUL TIME!
MMMPH!
JIM DAVIS
© 1987 United Feature Syndicate, Inc.
HOW WAS YOUR DATE?
I THINK I MADE AN IMPRESSION ON HER

GARFIELD, MEET THE NEWEST MEMBER OF OUR FAMILY, SWEETY BIRD
JIM DAVIS 3-30
I JUST KNOW YOU TWO ARE GOING TO GET ALONG FAMOUSLY, RIGHT, GARFIELD?
RIGHT. SURE. UH, WOULD YOU HAPPEN TO HAVE A LIGHT FOR MY CUTTING TORCH?

HELLO. I'M SWEETY BIRD. I SING SWEET HAPPY SONGS TO BRIGHTEN YOUR MORNING
BRIGHTEN MY MORNING?! DO YOU WANT TO BRIGHTEN MY MORNING?!
© 1987 United Feature Syndicate, Inc.
JIM DAVIS 3-31
THEN YOU CAN MARCH OUT OF THAT CAGE AND CRAWL BETWEEN TWO SLICES OF BREAD
JON!

GARFIELD, DO YOU LIKE SWEETY BIRD?
HE'S RIGHT UP THERE WITH DOGS AND MONDAYS

YOU WOULDN'T INTEND HIM ANY HARM, WOULD YOU?
I DON'T KNOW WHAT YOU'RE TALKING ABOUT

THEN WHY IS HE COVERED WITH CLAM SAUCE?
AN OLD FAMILY RECIPE
JIM DAVIS 4-1

SQUAWK!
JIM DAVIS 4-2

HONK!

DID WE REMEMBER HOW TO OPEN THE BIRD CAGE?
NOT ONLY THAT, WE FORGOT BIRDS COULD FLY

HEY, BIRD! YOU THINK YOU'RE SAFE OUT THERE, HUH?
WELL, I HAVE A LITTLE TREAT FOR YOU!
© 1987 United Feature Syndicate, Inc.
JIM DAVIS 4-3
HAVE YOU, PERCHANCE, EVER HEARD A CAT SCREAM?

HEY, GARFIELD! WHAT ARE YOU DOING OUT THERE?
AND LOOK! SWEETY BIRD'S ON YOUR HEAD!
JIM DAVIS 4-4
© 1987 United Feature Syndicate, Inc.
WHERE'S MY CAMERA?!
I LOATHE LIFE

HURRY, GARFIELD, THE TV WORKOUT SHOW IS ABOUT TO START!
YOU PROMISED YOU'D TRY IT. SO LET'S GO
OKAY, BUT FIRST ANSWER ME THIS...
JUST HOW THE HECK AM I SUPPOSED TO MOVE?
JIM DAVIS 4-6

OKAY, STAND UP STRAIGHT AND PUT YOUR HANDS ON YOUR HIPS
THOSE OF YOU TOO FAT TO FIND YOUR HIPS JUST GIVE IT YOUR BEST GUESS
I HATE SARCASTIC FITNESS INSTRUCTORS
© 1987 United Feature Syndicate, Inc.
JIM DAVIS 4-8

NOW FOR JUMPING JACKS ON THE TWO COUNT
JIM DAVIS 4-9
ONE!
CRASH!
OH, BY THE WAY, BEFORE WE GET TO TWO, DON'T TRY THIS EXERCISE ON A RECENTLY POLISHED FLOOR
NOW HE TELLS ME

THAT'S GOOD, EVERYBODY. PUSH UP!
...AND DOWN!
...AND UP!...
I WAS BUILT FOR PUSH-UPS
JIM DAVIS 4-10

NO, SERIOUSLY, LINDA, I'M A FUN GUY. I DO GREAT IMPRESSIONS!
YOU DO IMPRESSIONS TOO? LET'S HEAR ONE
LISTEN TO THIS, GARFIELD. SHE SOUNDS JUST LIKE A DIAL TONE!
THIS MAN HAS NO BRAIN
JIM DAVIS
4-11

DO YOU KNOW WHAT I HATE MOST ABOUT THIS BED?
UNNNGH!
TRYING TO SLEEP ON MY BACK
JIM DAVIS 4-15

© 1987 United Feature Syndicate, Inc.
SEE ANYTHING YOU LIKE?
JIM DAVIS 4-14

YOU'RE A SLOB, GARFIELD. WHY CAN'T YOU STAY AS CLEAN AS OTHER CATS?
GARFIELD

YOU'RE SUPPOSED TO WASH YOURSELF LIKE THIS
OH, VERY WELL
GARFIELD

START WITH THIS ARM AND MAKE IT SNAPPY. YOU HAVE A LOT OF TERRITORY TO COVER
GARFIELD
JIM DAVIS 4-13

THIN ICE
SPLOOSH!
THIN ICE
HEY! THIS ICE ISN'T THIN!
NEITHER ARE YOU
THIN ICE
JIM DAVIS 4-18

OH, NO! YOU CHEWED UP MY NEWSPAPER AGAIN!
JIM DAVIS 4-17
HEY! THIS ISN'T THE PAPER I GET. IT MUST BELONG TO A NEIGHBOR
© 1987 United Feature Syndicate, Inc.
KNOCK! KNOCK! KNOCK!
A 250 LB. NEIGHBOR, TO BE PRECISE

GARFIELD!
YOU SHREDDED MY RUNNING SHOES!
SOMEDAY YOU'LL THANK ME FOR THAT, JON
JOGGING'S THE DISEASE. I'M THE CURE
JIM DAVIS 4-7

IT'S TIME TO GET UP
JIM DAVIS 4-16
CREAK!
CRACK!
© 1987 United Feature Syndicate, Inc.
IT'S ALSO TIME TO GO ON A DIET

AH, I SEE JON PLACED A PIE ON THIS WINDOWSILL TO TEMPT ME
WELL, LET IT BE KNOWN I'M CAPABLE OF RESISTING ALL TEMPTATIONS!
I JUST DON'T CHOOSE TO
JIM DAVIS
5-2

I LOVE THIS FEELING OF POWER
JIM DAVIS 5-1
© 1987 United Feature Syndicate, Inc.
NOW I WANT TO WATCH A COOKING SHOW!
CLICK

JON! JON! WAKE UP! IT'S HORRIBLE! IT'S AWFUL! YOU GOTTA DO SOMETHING!

WHAT IS IT, GARFIELD?! IS THE HOUSE ON FIRE?! IS THERE A BURGLAR?!
WORSE!!!
© 1987 United Feature Syndicate, Inc.

I HAVE HUNGER PANGS!
JIM DAVIS 4-30

NOW I LAY ME DOWN TO SLEEP...
JIM DAVIS 4-29
HOLD THAT THOUGHT...
I THINK I HEARD GARFIELD OPEN THE REFRIGERATOR DOOR

I AM HUNGRY
GARFIELD
4-28
THEREFORE I AM
GARFIELD
RATIONALIZING ANOTHER BOUT WITH GLUTTONY, GARFIELD
I DON'T DISCUSS PHILOSOPHY WITH PEA BRAINS
JIM DAVIS
GARFIELD

IT WAS HIGH NOON WHEN THE STRANGER RODE INTO TOWN
4-27
JIM DAVIS

NOW COMES MY FAVORITE PART...

HE HITCHED UP HIS HORSE AND AMBLED INTO THE SALOON

SCREEEEE
AND JUST WHAT ARE YOU DOING?
JIM DAVIS 4-25

SWIPE!

YOUR TURN
YOU GOTTA JUSTIFY EVERYTHING, DON'T YOU?!

I ATE TOO MUCH
GARFIELD
JIM DAVIS 4-24
I'LL PROBABLY GET ANOTHER SERMON FROM JON
GARFIELD
GARFIELD, YOU EAT TOO MUCH
I WAS HOPING YOU WOULDN'T NOTICE

HERE COMES THE MAILMAN, GARFIELD. I WANT YOU TO BE ON YOUR BEST BEHAVIOR
JIM DAVIS
4-23
ROWRR!
© 1987 United Feature Syndicate, Inc.
I MUST ADMIT, THAT WAS ONE OF MY BETTER BEHAVIORS

HOW DID YOU GET TO BE SO LAZY, GARFIELD?
BRAINS, HARD WORK, TENACITY AND DEDICATION. YOU'RE NOT JUST BORN LAZY, YOU KNOW. IT'S AN ACQUIRED SKILL...
© 1987 United Feature Syndicate, Inc.
I'M SORRY I ASKED
...AN ART FORM, IF YOU WILL, NOT UNLIKE POETRY, DANCE OR MUSIC
JIM DAVIS 4·22

LIFE HAS MANY GOOD THINGS TO OFFER: MUSIC, ART, LITERATURE...
JIM DAVIS 4-21

SOMETIMES I THINK ABOUT EDUCATING MYSELF ON THOSE SUBJECTS...

BUT THEN I THINK, "STICK WITH WHAT YOU KNOW"
GARFIELD

THIS IS A PERFECT DAY TO STAY IN BED AND CONTEMPLATE LIFE'S TRUTHS
YIP! YIP!
GET UP, GARFIELD!
BRINNNNG!
© 1987 United Feature Syndicate, Inc.
TRUTHS LIKE: "MONDAYS STINK"
JIM DAVIS 4-20

AHA! SO JON'S TRYING TO SNEAK OFF ON VACATION WITHOUT ME, HUH?

HE'LL HAVE QUITE A SURPRISE IN STORE FOR HIM
© 1987 United Feature Syndicate, Inc.

WHO SAYS NOTHING GOOD EVER HAPPENS ON A MONDAY?
JIM DAVIS
5-4

LAZINESS AND PROCRASTINATION GO HAND IN HAND
SEE THIS HAIR?
IT'S CAT HAIR I NEVER GOT AROUND TO SHEDDING LAST YEAR
JIM DAVIS 5-5